UPLVL COMMUNICATION™

The Ultimate Solution to Save Relationships and Eliminate Hurtful, Damaging, & Meaningless Arguments

Kenya K. Stevens
Carl E. Stevens, Jr.

FIRST EDITION

ISBN: 978-1-7331648-0-1
Self-As-Source Publishing

Author: Kenya K. Stevens and Carl E. Stevens, Jr.
Published: September 2019

Web Address: https://www.progressiveloveacademy.com

CONTENTS

INTRODUCTION

*"The way we communicate with others and with our-
selves ultimately determines the quality of our lives"*
~ Anthony Robbins

The Objective of UPLVL Communication™ Is Sanity

I recall the days I sat paralyzed on my marital bed with thoughts
of committing violence acts against my husband. Negative images
whirling through my mind, taking me over; like so many daggers,
they cut my spirit apart. It wasn't that I wanted to kill him, my dear
husband, who'd dedicated his life to working with me as a business
partner, father to our three children, friend, and lover. It was that
I wanted to express myself and be solidly heard, solidly validated,
and simply acknowledged in my pain. I didn't know what I needed
then but, in hindsight, realize I wanted to be heard, seen, met, and
received in my emotion, but the way our communication was set
up didn't allow for it.

I hadn't seen an example of how to effectively communicate
the scary emotions; emotions like anger, rage, even hatred or fear.
I'd seen them expressed, no doubt, in my home growing up. But
I hadn't, to date, seen them received in grace.

My parents, whom I love and cherish, had done their level
best—with no tools, mind you—to move through life's challenges
together. When anger would flare, I saw physical violence and
verbal abuse. Yes, as I recall it, the only *goto* they had to release
the tension was violence. This is what I feared; I feared being
ineffective and, thus, unmet. I feared allowing anger to take over
my body and be left sitting in it, alone or, worse, ridiculed for it.

1

I also feared violence; in fact, I'd normalized this as part of any relationship, likely due to the examples I saw growing up. So, the fact that violence followed me into my marriage isn't mysterious.

As time passed, and one decade turned to two, I realized how very much my husband and I hurt one another, physically and mentally; and without effective tools, we would pass this on to our children. It wasn't a purposeful or directed pain we inflicted upon one another; it was subtle. I realized this communication issue wasn't simply *chemistry issues* between my husband and myself. This was a deep-rooted pattern of being unable to communicate effectively that I would eventually figure out plagued all my relationships, including familial, corporate, and friendships.

Each time I hit an emotional bump in the road, I found myself fuming, unable to speak until the pot in my mind was boiling over, at which time I might turn over a bookcase, lock my husband out of the house, or simply resort to throwing blows. I'd recall this is just as my parents did. Yet, each time it occurred, I began to study myself more closely, and being in the profession of supporting others as a relationships coach, I'd eventually work to explore my state of being and the series of events that led to each outburst.

Eventually, I began to recognize patterns and how they show up and take over. I eventually saw that the emotion I was experiencing wasn't the fullness of who I am and how I wanted to express. It was uncanny to note that the part of me experiencing the emotion was literally observable by another part of myself, maybe a watcher or processor. This seemingly higher element within me wasn't in the fray with me; rather, it watched as I became the fray. In other words, I was able to realize what my emotion was about, I was able to watch it and even have an opinion about it from a space outside of it!

This realization and splicing of myself was not, in and of itself, a way out of the emotion. But I simply found it curious that these seemingly twin elements existed within me. One part was out of control and backed up with unexpressed emotion; the other part was watching, listening, and observing. What could be the use and purpose of such a design?

Over time, I created a course called *The Trust Forum*, wherein students of *The Progressive Love Academy* could easily begin utilizing the observation post within as a companion to the emotional spaces we enter, naturally, as human conditions allot. Having both these energetics present was somehow a key.... So I'd have students begin to open the communication channel between these two *inner elements.*

Students began to report that when emotion attempts to take over, having a second inner element there, standing by, to first empathize deeply with the emotional state of the other inner element within, was helpful. For example: A student noted they were in rage about their boyfriend's adulterous affairs. The student was instructed to allow herself to rage and express in a private place and then to simulate *being heard* by the other inner element as a way to self-soothe.

This was immediately effective in taking the level of rage down from, say, a 10 to a 5. Just the act of simply acknowledging oneself IN the emotion was primarily responsible for reducing the level of emotional pain the student experienced.

My next course and curriculum would attempt to take this form of acknowledgement out of the self and into any relationship, following a system or dance of sorts, involving interplay of creating safe space to be witnessed in emotion, releasing emotion, and asking for the same kind of empathy the students once only expected and created within.

This led to the **UPLVL Communication**™ breakthrough:

Emotions must be heard by, catered to, and spoken with a Witness. This Witness must remain neutral in order to hear the emotion without taking it personal. This is the only way to allow a storm overhead to move through the body rather than become stuck within it.

UPLVL Communication ™ is a system of utilizing specific steps in communicating powerful emotions that might otherwise seethe within and eventually explode or implode, causing illness in relationships. As a coach, I have held firmly in mind the evolution of our modern, Western, culture; emotion has been something to hold in, ignore, keep hidden and feel shame about. *UPLVL* promotes the release of the entire cultural paradigm such that we can finally become vulnerable again with anyone at any time without feeling weak, unseen, and disruptive.

In part one of the exploration into this innovative system, we dive into the precepts, what must be understood about the culture we've grown around us based on our learnings from media, schools, and community. We provide a new way of viewing the world and ourselves so that we can effectively command new processes in our delivery and receiving of speech, language, and meaning.

In part two of the book we dive into the four gateways of language, the very origins of thought:

- The Ego or Animal and how to integrate the powerful force of emotion back into our lives in a safe and reliable container.
- The Higher Self and how to process, hear, and acknowledge the language of peace within us.
- Ownership and what it means to take full command of our communication, emotions, and expressions thereof.
- Finally, Gratitude, how to view life's challenges and feel a new sense of gracious acceptance of any and all scenarios we might

find ourselves in visa vie language and speech, the very benchmark of relationship.

You'll receive from this work a graceful dance where communication becomes extraordinarily simple. With each new *dance move*, you learn adding to the beauty of your language, communication, processing, and embodiment! You'll be able to express anything to anyone without fear of rejection, emotional abandonment, discomfort, or fear. The dance of sublime communication you discover has always been possible and wants to happen effortlessly in your life and relationships. Now you'll have learned each move to precision and have obtained the possibility of stringing the moves together to create harmony in your home, office, family, corporation, or community!

The Greatest Lie Ever Told

We've been lied to. All these years, we've been told that the main reasons for failed relationships are bad finances and communication problems when nothing can be further from the truth. A lack of money doesn't break up a couple who once proclaimed a profound love for each other, but character issues certainly can. Saying that finances or lack thereof is the cause for failed marriages is like saying the existence of food is the reason for obesity. What the relationship "experts" really meant to say was that lies and deceits, which were exposed in financial matters, are the cause of breakups. Or maybe it was a lack of empathy for their partner's shortcomings and addictions, which caused them to consistently prioritize soothing their own pain over the physical needs of the family, that causes marriages to break down. Money isn't the root of all evil, but in a capitalistic society, money will certainly expose our true character. Money will indicate where our strengths and weaknesses are when it comes to things like discipline, managing stress and anxiety, being goal-oriented and purpose-driven, and our ability to manage our addictions and pain. Money plays a significant role in our marriages and relationships, but money, by itself, has no power over us, especially whenever real love and commitment are present. That's just the truth of the matter.

What about communication? Isn't the fact that most don't know how to communicate with one another causing these relationships to fail? No. We communicate just fine. When I ask where the peanut butter is, you have no question about what I'm referring to or what I want. When you ask me what time it is, I know exactly what you mean and respond in kind. When you say you love me or when I say "I like you," you know exactly what that implies. If you look at most couples, the communication is, at worst functional and, at best, exceptional. People live out their relationships and marriages doing everything from paying bills, coordinating child pickups from school, organizing weekend activities and vacations, to planning meals for the week. They file joint taxes and open retirement accounts, both of which take tremendous coordination and communication skills. Trust me, we communicate quite nicely, but what we don't do a good job at is: (a) telling our own authentic truths and (b) recognizing the source of our feelings, wants, and needs. This is the true source of relationships, business partnerships and marriages breaking up at epic proportions, and that's great news because, at least, we know that language classes aren't necessary to fix our communication issues. No need to repeat our high school language arts classes.

Therefore, we do need some support being able to say what's authentic! We need courses in expressing what is actually on our hearts. We also need help reconciling our feelings against unrealistic expectations and the fantasy of romantic relationships and marriage. We don't need better, basic, communication skills; we need the courage and awareness to reclaim our lives and speak and act authentically, even if it means others will be hurt by it. We can never control how others feel or react. We can never control what authentically feels good to us or when change strikes and causes us to shift direction in life. Why feel shame about the inevitable? Why feel shame about having human feelings, thoughts, and emotions? Why feel shame about genuine wants and desires that are innate to your DNA as an incarnated human being? This is what the relationship experts should have told you, that you're ashamed of the truth of how you feel and you fear telling your partner (i.e., communications issues) out of shame and guilt.

This is why UPLVL Communication™ is critical for our relationships because we need a tool to assist us with having the truly hard conversations that wouldn't happen otherwise. We need a container for truth and authenticity so that we can stay within our power as individuals and couples. Who can we really tell our authentic truth to? How do we even have those conversations? UPLVL Communication™ provides exactly that container and structure for real conversation and communication.

"People fail to get along because they fear each other; they fear each other because they don't know each other; they don't know each other because they have not communicated with each other."

~ Martin Luther King Jr.

Part 1 – Foundation & Prerequisites

The Progressive Love™ Philosophy

As with any set of tools we use, whether physical or process-based, we must first established the conditions by which those tools will be utilized in order for them to have maximum effectiveness, as well as the philosophical premise supporting their use. The premise for the UPLVL Communication™ toolset is the Progressive Love™ philosophy, which essentially says — *"I Create My Life."* It's the concept that we take one-hundred percent accountability for our lives. Why? Because we have one-hundred percent of the power to do it and whether we're aware of it or not, we're creating our lives every single second of every day. **The Progressive Love™** philosophy is one of personal empowerment and gives us the best opportunity to find the peace, happiness, and fulfillment we desire, regardless of how that may look to us.

Let's break down how the concept of Progressive Love™ and personal empowerment go together. If I come into the realization and understanding that I have all the power and innate capabilities to shape my life in the image of my desire, then what I've also come into the realization of is complete *self-love*. Actually, I would change the definition of *self-love* from merely a regard for one's own happiness to the realization that "I am all I need in life." That's not to say I don't need others to support me through life, but the idea that I, myself, can literally extract those critical resources from others and the environment; this is the *Progressive* concept of self-love.

Why do people tend to get down on themselves? Failure, fear, hopelessness or the perception that we've come up short in a particular area of life and, therefore, must not be enough and therefore aren't worthy of love from others or self. However, when we realize that failure in life isn't a lack of personal capability, but instead a process of learning to use the tools we've been given to create our lives, we no longer doubt the essence of who we are. Instead, we take the opportunity to learn more about ourselves. Failure isn't a reflection of unworthiness, but an indication that we have powers within us that we've yet to tap into. It's simply the realization that we've let a part of our greatness lay dormant; but now, it's time to wake it up.

How about hopelessness? Most of the time, hopelessness comes from a belief that what we need is outside of ourselves. The money, knowledge, resources, time, or talents are somewhere out there beyond our reach; therefore, we have no hope. In that moment, we can fall into despair and give up on our goals and ourselves. What follows may be depression or even self-abuse as a subconscious act to punish the unworthy — us. Or perhaps, we begin to experience a pain beyond bearing and resign ourselves to opioids, intoxicants, or reckless behavior as a means to remove the feelings of hurt. What if we felt assured that there is always hope in all scenarios in life? What if we clearly felt as though there is always a way, even if that way isn't logical or familiar to us? Even if that way takes us through a path unknown, scary, or treacherous?

It's true the money may not be in our bank account right now, but it doesn't mean we can't meet our obligations or acquire an asset. There's always another way and the understanding of that way is inside of you, even if it's in the form of knowing who to contact to provide that specific information. This is precisely how we define self-love via the Progressive Love™ philosophy — the ability to know one has the power to manifest and/or create what is needed in life.

Knowing fully and embracing completely that we create our

lives and that the power to make something new is squarely within us is self-love. Now we can remain optimistic and hopeful. Now we know that we're always capable, which means we never need to not value our worth again. It's never about whether we're good enough. It's always about learning a new way or finding a new, indwelling talent to achieve our goals. It's as simple as noting the difference between *knowing* you're enough, but not understanding how to move forward versus believing you lack the "success gene."

True self-love changes the game for all of us as human beings forever. The fact that we're worthy and capable becomes a constant and now life becomes a beautiful, complex puzzle to figure out. Yes, it can be scary at times. Yes, fear will rear its ugly head, but what's wrong with fear? Fear becomes beautiful to those who achieve true *self-love* because it tells us what part of the journey is new for us and which indwelling character traits need more practice and development. Don't we want to know the parts of us that need further attention, healing, or development? Don't we want an emotional signal to give us a clear indication that we have the opportunity to get better? I say, yes. I want to know my strengths and weaknesses before I take the journey so that the necessary adjustments and growth can be made. Fear is nothing to fear, but it's an emotional gift to us all. The misinterpretation that the feeling of fear means we're somehow incapable is flawed logic. Finally, defining *self-love* is a progressive way to support us in deeply loving ourselves as spiritual and human beings with all the power and capabilities to create our best life. That's what we mean when we say "Progressive Love." Progressive, empowering thoughts and beliefs that support us in loving ourselves on the highest level possible without question, condition, or apology – Progressive Love™.

The "I" in I Create My Life means that we are the center of our lives and Universe. It means no one outside of us has the power to ultimately shape or influence our lives. "Create" means that we're made in the likeness of that which created us. We ourselves are creators, and that's exactly what we do every second of every day. "My" means I take responsibility for it all. Any and everything I experience in life is me. It is mine and I take complete ownership for it all. The focus is never about others. It's never about what they're doing or not doing but, instead, what I'm doing. "Life" denotes the entirety of our existence from our very first incarnation to our last breath and beyond. If we're involved in it, then we've created it and it's our life.

The big question, of course, is "How can I be responsible for the entire world?" Better yet, "How can I be responsible for someone else and their choices? That just doesn't seem fair." I would say the real question is, "Why not be responsible for the entire world?" Why would that be a source of tension for anyone? Is it because of our judgments of the world? Is the world an awful place? Well, I'll leave that judgment to you, but, for me, I accept it as my creation. How do we experience the world? Exactly — through our senses. We see something and then make a determination of what we saw. In other words, we pass judgment on it. The truth is, we don't have any real experience or interaction with 99.99% of the world. We don't know what's really happening with ourselves half the time let alone anyone else, but our Ego tells us we know what's going on and whether or not we like it. But if we think about it, we can see how this is folly. Again, it's hard enough understanding our own experience let alone attempting to understand someone else's.

So how can we really know what's happening with anyone else or the rest of the world? We can't. Yes, it's true we can choose to accept someone else's interpretation of what others are going through or thinking, but again, second- and third-hand information is far from knowledge. But what I do know is my perception of what I'm sensing. I do know my reactions to and feelings about what my senses are telling me and I have complete control over them. The truth is, the world is completely and totally in my head, existing as a set of memories and interpretations of my sensory inputs, and my feelings of those interpretations shape my view and experience of this thing that we call the world. That, I do know. Are things actually happening out there somewhere? Sure. Do people have feelings, thoughts, and experiences? Yes. Does it appear that people are experiencing pleasure and pain and everything in between? That's what my brain is telling me, so yes! Are my interpretations actually true? Well, I know I'd like to think so, and I'm not here to tell anyone that their experiences aren't real, so let's just say that your interpretations are one-hundred percent real and true to you, and, for the purposes of interacting with our partners and creating our happiness, that's all that counts. So, let's agree to focus on our perceptions, judgments, and feelings as a foundation for improving our relationships; but we need to go a bit deeper.

So we've established the actual definition of self-love, and that the world is as we perceive it, but what is the basis for our perceptions? Meaning, what is possible for each of us to actually perceive? Wolfgang van Goethe [1749-1832] said, "We only see what we know." Another way to say it is, we can only see what our "story" allows us to see. Our stories are our collective memories, experiences, and thought processing capabilities, and they form the foundation of how we make sense of every single experience we have in life. It's similar to language where, in order to understand it, we must have a context (i.e., experience) with it so that we can tell ourselves what it means, how to feel about it, and how to react accordingly. Without that context, we won't even be able to hear the words that are being spoken to us. True, we may hear sounds, but we won't hear those sounds in the context of words, sentences, and paragraphs. We also won't hear them based on their proper enunciation. We've seen this in neurological experiments when a distorted recording of someone saying something is played, but isn't recognizable in the least. However when the original recording, with no distortion, is played, we are suddenly able to hear the words inside of the distorted recording going forward. Why? Because the brain has a story for that distorted recording now. It has a foundation and we can hallucinate or fill in the reality that will allow us to now hear (i.e., understand) the distorted recording.

The more you study the latest neurological data, the more it can be surmised that we're actually hallucinating our realities. Meaning, what we perceive in our environment is largely a combination of sensory inputs and brain filler (i.e., illusion). Interesting stuff. The degree to which we fill in reality will continue to be disputed and studied in psychology and neuroscience for decades, but we do know it happens. In other words, it's a fact that the brain fills in reality for things such as side vision, events and objects we haven't experienced before, things that are far away and difficult to sense, and especially things that are beyond a comfortable level of sensation and perception like our internal organs. Maybe this is what Edgar Allen Poe meant when he said, "All that we see or seem is but a dream within a dream." In other words, what we see is a hallucination. What we think we are is a hallucination as well.

What's the implication of the fact that we're having individual perceptions? First, we can agree that what we generally call reality is actually the "common perception" of two or more people. Meaning, if we all have the same story from which to perceive reality, we'll all generate the same visual images of what that reality is and thus agree. Second, our individual stories are the primary component feeding into what and how we perceive in the world. This is why two people from different financial upbringings won't be able to see money and wealth in the same way, even when taking the same finance and economics classes. Thirdly, if we're hallucinating reality, it means everything we experience is subjective. In other words, there is no absolute quality to describe any particular thing in the world. You might say the sky is blue, and I might say it's teal. Lastly, from that standpoint, there's no "out there" outside of me per se, but rather only and primarily "in here" inside of my head that's actually projecting my story of what's out there. Interesting concepts, no doubt, and plenty to think about.

In summary, in order to live in boundless *self-love*, create the life you desire, and communicate effectively, you'll have to realize you're coming from a very personal perspective that certainly isn't one-hundred percent shared with anyone else including those around you, but might also be less than ten percent of how they see it. We need to make sure we're not talking about two different realities (i.e., hallucinations) if there's any hope of creating effective communication.

> *"Emotional awareness is necessary so you can properly convey your thoughts and feelings to the other person."*
> – Jason Goldberg

The Progressive Love™ Tenets

The purpose of any tenet is to support the individual in living within the goals and objectives of the particular philosophy, lifestyle, or religion they choose. The same is true of the *Progressive Love™ Tenets*, which are designed to support the individual in staying firmly within the Progressive Love™ Philosophy and, thus, in line with self-love — the ability to create one's life. We're not talking

15

laws or rules, in which anyone has the right to come down on you for violating a specific modality of behavior. These are simply guides that help us see where we are within our empowerment and ability to take full accountability for our lives. If we "violate" a tenet, it simply means we weren't in our most empowered position relative to creating the life we desire. The Progressive Love™ Tenets are as follows:

- No Victims, No Villains
- No Shame, No Blame
- No Cop Outs, No Drop Outs
- The Purpose is Growth, The Benefit is Love
- I Create My Life

No Victims, No Villains

Here's where the rubber hits the proverbial road. This tenet states there are no victims in the world and conjunctly, there are no villains. Victims and villains are two sides of the same coin because one cannot exist without the other. What is a victim? A victim is a person who was tricked, duped, harmed, or injured as a result of the intentional action of another person (i.e., villain). It's someone who became the casualty of another person's actions whose sole intent was to further their self materially, emotionally, or psychologically. At the very least, a villain is someone who doesn't have our best interest at heart and demonstrates that via their actions. Another aspect of the definition of victimhood is a person who doesn't have the power or ability to avoid being the victim because they lack the physical strength, intellectual knowledge, or biological development to thwart the villain. This is closer to the modern use of the word *victim* — a state of powerlessness of the abused. Are their people who assault, hurt, and abuse others? Yes. Are their people who take advantage of an individual's class, gender, race, ethnicity, lack of understanding, or desperate circumstances? Yes. So, how are they not victims and the assailants not villains? Let's attempt to answer that question indirectly.

Inside the I Ching oracle commentary is a saying — "Everything serves to further." There is yet another saying we've coined in Progressive Love™- "Nothing is against me." In the Christian faith, they say — "No weapon formed against me shall prosper." In a modern context, these sayings don't seem to make any sense. If a person takes your money at gunpoint, haven't they "formed a weapon against you"? Haven't they prospered? Aren't they the villain in this example and aren't you the victim? Again, we are free to look at it this way, but the Progressive Love™ philosophy says that we ultimately grew from that experience. We became better, stronger, and smarter as a result. We became more aware of our environment and surroundings. We became more in touch with our carelessness and inability to pick up on environmental indicators that may have warned us if we had been paying closer attention. The question is, would every person on the planet have been robbed at gunpoint and had all their money taken? No. Some people wouldn't have trusted the feel or vibe of the situation and chosen a different route home. Some people are aware of self-defense or the use of weapons to protect themselves or their loved ones and may have thwarted the attack. Is it possible to have the knowledge and awareness to protect not only ourselves in the future but also our children and elders in the family and community? Is it possible that we can now pass on the knowledge for others to not only avoid being robbed, but perhaps save their lives or that of others if something similar or worse were to happen to them? Please note that we're not talking about guilt here because that's a judgment and outside of the context of this discussion. What we're asking is this: do these life experiences actually "serve to further" our life and development? The answer is, of course, yes. Of course, every life situation gives us powerful lessons to help us navigate our future. Everything that we experience serves to further us in some way, but we don't take it that way because we often feel hurt by the experience itself. We may experience physical pain as a result of the attack. We may experience a permanent injury or scar as a result of the attack, and that doesn't feel good. But that's just life. It's rare that we leave this incarnation without any battle scars, and if we don't put a judgment on what these scars or permanent handicaps mean but, rather, accept them as a part of the lesson of that we experience, it will be easier for us to move on in gratitude and appreciation. Didn't the robber benefit? They got the money, right? They didn't get caught by the police, right? Aren't they a villain for violating another human being? Sure, we can label them a villain if that makes us feel better, but I wouldn't rush to judgment that they benefited in the way we think they did. Is having to rob others for survival the best use of their power and potential? Could they be a talented artist or computer programmer who has avoided developing their talents to create a better life? Is living in a constant state of fear of the police a benefit? Does hurting others take them deeper into their unresolved childhood pain and put them further on a path of violence, uncertainty, and pain? It's hard to answer these questions, but I think we would all agree that their potential is largely going untapped in other areas of their life and their ability to hurt others is an indication of unresolved traumas that need immediate attention. So are they a villain, are they the real victim, or are they a teacher? We know they're a teacher because if we can get past a victim mindset, hurt, and confusion from the event, we can most certainly come out better than we were before it happened. So are there victims and villains or students and teachers?

From another perspective, we can't understand No Victims, No Villains without being in touch with our stories. Because our stories will tell us what a victim is versus what a villain is. Our stories will tell us what a real opportunity is versus a dead end. They say, "One person's trash is another person's treasure." I wonder how that could be because trash is trash, right? Just like a villain is a villain and a victim is a victim, right? It's also said, "What's good for the goose is also good for the gander." I love all these sayings because they communicate such deep wisdom in the simplest terms that even a grade school student can understand. How can what's good for the villain also be what's good for the victim? It makes you wonder. Isn't it possible to put two people into the same situation and one person come out wealthy and the other come out in abject poverty? Why is that when the situation *is what it is?* It's like some investors making a ton of money on a down market while others lose their shirts. What's your story about opportunity, growth, and creating your life? I've known people who had what most people would define as horrific things happen to them only to become some of the most powerful and influential people on the planet. I guess their story was different when it came to "traumatic" events. I guess they saw the opportunity to turn lemons into lemonade. Our story creates our lives and how we perceive our lives. To perceive them differently, we simply need to change our story and perspective. Simple as that. So, yes, we can choose to see ourselves as victims to life, politics, relationship drama, lies, deceit, and societal inequalities, or we can find the opportunities that lie within. Again, there's nothing telling us not to view the world on our specific terms. It's up to you. From a Progressive Love™ perspective, we focus on the benefit of all of life's events as well as how we created them and we use that knowledge to refine our ability to become more powerful creators. It's really just a choice. So are there victims and villains? Yes, if you want there to be, but for those who choose empowerment as their lifestyle, the answer is unequivocally — No!

No Shame, No Blame

In a culture of villains and victims, we always get to play both roles regardless of how good a person we think we are or how considerate we function toward our neighbors. The role of villain is an assigned one, either by you or those who consider themselves the victim. Both the villain and victim assignments are completely subjective; meaning, if your neighbor believes you're playing your music too loud, then you're the villain, according to them. Or if we have a different political affiliation than the "correct" one, whatever that is, we're on an entire team of villains. If our spouse believes we were mean to them or said hurtful things or weren't fair then, again, we're labeled the villain. See how it works? Not fair, I know, but that's what victim and villain culture looks like. Completely random, completely subjective, and without the necessity of agreement from anyone. Actually, one reason victim and villain culture is so popular is because we can just assign ourselves the victim at any time in hopes of gaining sympathy or attention from others. We can also easily castigate others and hurt them when they've upset us. This feels really good in the moment but isn't empowering in the least; but to each their own.

What happens when we assign ourselves as the villain because we perceived that we've made a mistake or hurt others? Or maybe we just have a side to us that others universally accept as confrontational or bad and we accept that assessment. That's when shame can enter the picture. When we unintentionally hurt others and they assign us as the villain, we're often conditioned to feel bad about our actions. We shame ourselves. "Why did I do that?" "I should have known better." "I'm such an asshole sometimes." "I'm a failure." The conditioning starts when we're children and do something wrong and are subsequently reprimanded for it. "Why did you color the wall with the crayons?!" "You ruined your new clothes!" "You lost your winter coat again!" "You didn't eat your vegetables like I asked you too!" "You failed your quiz. Take it home and have your parents sign it so they can see you haven't been doing your work." The list goes on. The *culture of shame* (victim and villains) causes us to summon the feeling associated with shame, which is depression, guilt, and doubt. Then, to avoid those feelings, we begin to shape our lives such that shame and the associated emotions can be avoided because of how painful they feel. How do we avoid shame? Simple, avoid being the villain. Avoid hurting other people. Avoid taking risks and doing what feels great when it's not popularly accepted, all in the name of playing it safe (i.e., not being the villain). Who wants that label, right?

Who wants a villain label in a victim culture? No one wants it. Instead, we look for ways to become the victim because that's more popular and brings the sympathy and attention we seek. It gives us a pass and allows us to move more freely throughout society. If we've been given the victim label, then we're victims. We've been wronged and given a raw deal, and that's not fair. The opposite is true for the villain label. Things get tough when you're labeled the villain. People don't trust you or don't want you around because they don't want to be associated with a villain. Or they're fearful of becoming one of your victims. So, what are our choices if we've been labeled the villain?

- Work hard as hell to show that we're not the villain and hope-fully, over time, people will forgive us.
- Accept the villain role, and do more of what we've been doing to hurt people because that's who we are according to society.
- Feel badly about being the villain and begin self-sabotaging our lives by thinking less of ourselves than is the actual case.
- Cause ourselves immense pain by punishing ourselves with guilt and shame. Then perhaps take pain killers or practice destructive behavior to take our minds off of what we think about ourselves. The cycle then repeats.

What's the point or benefit in this? No one is a villain, but these subjective assignments can truly turn us into one, for real. No one is bad and no one is doing anything "wrong" according to the Progressive Love™ Tenets. We are all simply acting out our stories while reacting to others who are doing the same.

The same holds true when we intentionally harm or hurt another person. Because we haven't been taught to transmute painful energy, we often pass the pain we're feeling onto others. For example, if someone hurts our feelings, we either feel badly (i.e., shame) or we lash out at the ones who hurt us or others we feel are powerless against us (i.e., bullying). It's not that it's really in our hearts to hurt others, but we're in pain and feel better when we see others suffering with us. Misery loves company, right? But when we pass that hurt onto others, we feel badly for doing so because now someone is suffering because of us, and that doesn't feel good to most people. The shame sets in again. Does it mean we won't hurt them again? No it doesn't, but we won't feel good about it nonetheless. This feeling will be compounded when others bear witness to the pain we've caused and label us the villain. Again, shame is the result, and we take steps to escape the pain of being associated with the villain label. The cycle repeats. We should never feel shame about what we've done or who we are. If we want to change our behavior — fine. If we want to support someone who we perceive as being in a worse position because of something we've done or said — fine. But don't do it because of shame or guilt. Don't do it because you're a bad person; you're not. Supporting someone else won't change the story in their head about what a victim or villain is. It won't change how they feel about their self. It won't boost their self-esteem. It just won't. If we support someone else, we must do it because it's what we sincerely want to do. We must do it from a place of love and authenticity, not shame; otherwise, it's meaningless because we didn't mean it anyway and would only do it to lift the hurt off our own hearts. What's the point? The shame remains. The purpose of the second tenet of Progressive Love™- No Shame, No Blame — is to remove the concept of shame such that we can operate authentically and heal ourselves of the very story of shame to become more grounded in self-love.

Of course, if I'm the victim, it's because someone (the villain) did something to me, which means they're to blame. Blame is always assigned to the villain because it's only given when we feel we or someone else has been violated in some way. Blame is the opposite of giving credit because credit usually has a positive connotation. Blaming isn't a powerful act because it means we've assigned someone the villain and someone else, usually us, the victim. We're back at square one. We remain in the habit of avoiding accountability for how we're feeling and how we process those feelings. Blaming keeps us in the habit of not analyzing our stories and applying self-love — shifting our realities! We're back to not accepting that we have stories creating our perceptions. We must accept that we have stories about ourselves and the world, in general, and that these stories are defining what a victim or villain is and what emotions should accompany each of those subjective designations.

Let's walk through what we're saying here because this isn't about denying reality or any specific actions by ourselves or others but, rather, our *judgment* of them. If someone hits you while you're sitting at a stop light, for example, it's easy to assign yourself the victim and them the villain. In other words, it's easy to blame them for causing the accident; and from a fiscal perspective, it's important to blame them because the villain pays the money and the victim receives it. Because we live in a capitalistic culture, there will always be a financial component to all these designations; more on that later. We don't need to assign blame to be compensated when someone rear-ends us in a car. Instead, we simply assign reparation responsibility to the person who damaged the car. What if you were hurt in the accident? Again, the person will take responsibility for causing you bodily harm by paying for medical bills through their insurance company. Are you a victim? No, you just got hit by a car and guess what — these types of things happen in life. Sometimes, we're minding our own business and get hit or are set back by the actions of another person.

What if the person who hit you refuses to take responsibility for hitting you or perceives that you were responsible for the damage to your car? Are they the villain? No. They're someone with a different perception or opinion than you. They have a different philosophy that they live by. Maybe they are capitalists and believe in never voluntarily giving away money at their own expense. Sounds unfair, but it's really just a life philosophy and, trust me, many people live by it. You would never participate in something like that, right? Incorrect. You never know what you will or will not do. If you rear-end someone and your lawyer comes to you and says, not only can I help you avoid having to pay money, but I can get you five million dollars in damages, you might very well take him up on the offer, especially if the financial settlement comes from the insurance company and not the driver you rear-ended. Again, I'm not judging whether you would or wouldn't do something, but we're often quick to say what we won't do without having been in that situation. Most people in our culture tend to avoid blame because of the financial and emotional cost of accepting it. It's just something to think about.

In essence, blame and shame is a dead-end, shortcut to releasing 100% responsibility for one's life. If I can blame someone else for the misfortune I feel I've experienced, then I don't have to look deeply within to apply the "I Create My Life" sentiment of Progressive Love; thereby, I also avoid cultivating self-love. Yes. There's a trade-off for utilizing shame and/or blame in life scenarios. We forfeit our own power and autonomy. We forfeit the development of our ability to perceive ourselves as the center of the Universe, and creator therein. It may seem prudent to find the culprit, and of course shame or blame him or her, but when does it become more prudent to decipher what life is teaching us, and what powers we can develop in the aftermath of any possibility? Progressive Love™ designs a way to place oneself in the center of one's Universe for the purpose of becoming powerful in any experience and then creating ways to evolve past the pattern of having the same misfortunes repeatedly in life.

No Cop Outs, No Drop Outs

One of my favorite motivational speakers is David Goggins. He tells a story of being in the military and going through brutal water endurance training exercises taking place over a six-week period. This training was especially tough for him because he hated the water and couldn't swim. After the third week, he was called into the medical office and told he had sickle cell anemia, which is a dangerous blood condition that plagues a number of African-Americans. In that moment, he felt like a victim of bad genetics and a raw deal, but at the same time felt good that he wouldn't have to continue the training because it was kicking his ass. Again, being the victim, even of life circumstances, has its advantages because people will often give us a pass and take it easy on us. However, in this case, he surprisingly wasn't given a pass! He was told that he could still do the training because the sickle cell wasn't any more or less life threatening while going through the training. When he went back and reported his situation to the head trainer, he was told that he could get back into the training, but he would have to start from week one because he missed too much time compared to the rest of his platoon. Instead of going back into the training, he opted to drop out of it. In other words, he quit. He used his medical condition as a way to get out of the water training exercises. That's what we call dropping out. We find an excuse to remove ourselves from a situation we had previously committed ourselves to. Later Goggins realized that if he had gone through the complete training, he would have overcome his inner fears about water as well as his proclivity to quit on himself and not reach his potential.

What do we do when being the victim doesn't offer us enough advantages in life? We either drop out or we cop out of the situation. Why? Because, in our minds, we're the victim and deserve more consideration than we're being given by society or our partner or whoever; therefore, we're going to take matters into our own hands and resign. We see this in all areas of life, but especially in relationships where one partner isn't happy with what the other partner is doing and decides to leave. But why are they leaving? Is it because they don't love them anymore? Is it because the original commitment and intent of the relationship was renegotiated? No, because once you love someone that love never goes away; although, it can be buried below layers and layers of resentment and hurt. They're leaving because they don't have the solution or skills to fix the situation and, instead, quit. Or they want their partner to feel their hurt, so they leave them as a way to hurt them. That will show them, right? "How does that feel to be left alone!?" "What will you tell your mother and friends?" "You should have given me what I wanted. You really messed up this time. Now change your relationship status to 'Single' because I already have on my social media profiles."

Dropping out is the act of physically removing ourselves from a situation that we had previously committed to. It's the equivalent of walking out of the operating room halfway through a heart surgery you're performing on a patient. Extreme example? Maybe so, but let's not underestimate the impact of our choices, not only on others, but ourselves. Are we walking away from an opportunity to be in our power and tap into a communication or accountability talent that has previously lain dormant? It's hard to say, but if we see a pattern of dropping out of life, whether it be work, relationship, or school, we may want to examine it closer.

If dropping out is the physical resignation from life, relationships, and previous commitments, then copping out is the mental equivalent. It's staying physically, but not engaging mentally and emotionally. We see this in relationships a lot when people say, "I'll stay for the kids, but I refuse to engage my partner in any meaningful way." We also see this in career where people say, "I'll stay at the job for the money and do the bare minimum, but I'm not going to be an asset or innovator for the company." These actions seem justified until someone does it to us without us knowing about it. It's like bringing a car to the shop for repairs with a coupon for a twenty-percent discount and the mechanic decides to cut corners and use the cheapest parts available because we're not paying full price. This wouldn't feel good. Many of us have been in relationships with a partner who has copped out and is basically just going through the motions. So, they're with us because maybe they're living in our house but have no intentions on staying with us long term and we have no idea. They're looking for other partners while they're with us; meanwhile, we're making long-term plans to spend the rest of our lives with them. This is one of the greatest fears in relationships and a big complaint we see from a number of people — that they'll put in one-hundred percent into the relationship, but their partner will only give fifty percent. What makes this especially tough is that it's sometimes hard to see when someone has copped out of the relationship or work; whereas, dropping out is crystal clear because they're physically gone.

Some will say that dropping out is justified. What if I'm being physically abused and decide to leave my partner? Your physical safety is always a priority, but so is your mental and emotional safety. Sometimes, we tend to prioritize the physical over the psychological when both are critically important to maintaining balance in our lives. If your partner is physically abusive, it would be a great idea to put some space between you and them for safety sake. Separation is a great option for anyone who feels that they're taking on more than they should in a relationship, regardless of other people's judgments about it. However, separation doesn't have to be the end of a relationship or marriage. Usually the initiator of physical violence is someone dealing with mental and emotional issues and needs psychological support immediately. Therapy and support groups or even medication may be great options. The point is, we're not dropping out when we separate from our partners while they seek help for a potential mental illness. Leaving someone we love without at least exploring ways to bring balance back to the relationship is resignation, quitting, and giving up, especially when we're talking about committed marriage or life partnership. It's not just about breaking commitments and giving up when the going gets tough. It's also the fact that love never dies, as I stated earlier. You don't fall out of love with your partner. You don't lose love for them. Feelings don't change. What changes is we're exposed to new emotions and feelings based on new experiences with our partners, and those feelings, usually based on fear, take priority because we're programmed to avoid pain at all costs (just as we're taught to avoid being in the villain role). The love is still there, but the fear is stronger. The uncertainty running in conjunction with the memories of past relationships strike fear into our hearts and the natural fight or flight response is to fly away. That's all it is. What happened to forever? What happened to being in love and fighting for one another? The going got rough, tough, and scary and who wants that? Our stories were presented to us front and center and we chose to be the victim, blame our partner or circumstance, and drop out of the relationship. It's a pattern of behavior. It's a story. It's not real, but changeable, optional, and dynamic in nature. Fear has no authority over our lives unless we allow it too. It's just a story.

So in summary, the Progressive Love™ Tenet — No Cop Outs, No Drop Outs — means that we simply love. We love forever. Relationships may transition in nature, but they exist forever. It's easier to consider this an option if we refrain from depending on shame and blame, or upon victim and villain thinking as a basis for love or the choice not to love. This is only important when we consider the facts — the overall purpose of relating.

The Purpose is Growth

From our very inception as human and spiritual beings in the world, one constant is always at play in our lives — *growth*. One cell then two then four. Two feet tall to three. Twenty pounds to fifty. Knowing our ABCs to writing an essay. From needing others to provide for us to us providing for ourselves and others. From thinking we know what life is about to knowing we have zero idea. From a living, breathing organism to the dust that will give life to the next set of organisms. The cycle continues and all along the way, we're growing in knowledge, wisdom, and experience that we may or may not choose to apply to our lives. The point is, we're always growing and expanding. We are always experiencing something that we've never been exposed to and somehow, someway those experiences make us more, bigger, better, greater, and closer to our creator, whomever that may be for you. We're always advancing forward in the cycle of life regardless of how we judge our place within that advancement. Even as we become potentially debilitated as elders with a loss in flexibility, we are a year past where we were before. Therefore, we can say that the purpose isn't only growth, but expansion, experience, and advancement. The only constant is movement (i.e., change).

The same is true for relationships because each one is teaching us something new about ourselves, life, and people in general. Even when we're with the same person for fifty years, we're still learning about ourselves along the way and, hopefully, growing and becoming better versions of ourselves. If we're able to approach life and relationships from that perspective, then we can have compassion for ourselves and others along the way. We can actually find patience with ourselves because we know inherently that everyone is growing and learning. As a culture, we're not there yet (and there actually is no "there") as we always have more to learn; thus, we can expect to have challenges along our journey. A challenge is what most call a problem. However, when utilizing The Progressive Love™ Tenets and tools, employing self-love, we begin to release the concept of problems and embrace them as challenges or opportunities to grow. We can expect to make a mess of things along the way because it's always the first time. Our varied experiences may be similar, but they're always unique in their respective qualities. There is a saying: *variety breeds intelligence,* but what kind of variety? Variety of experience. What defines a new experience?

Experience is a simple formula:

$$(\text{Time} \times \text{Space}) \times \text{You}_x = \text{Experience}_x$$

Time represents whatever marker we'd like to use to represent where we are relative to other time dynamics. Space represents our location in the ever changing cosmos at any given point in time. You_x represents where and who we have grown to be at any particular point in time and space. Experience is the combination of these dynamics.

Since we're never in the same time, each experience is completely new and unique, and because change is a constant in the Universe, no space is ever the same, even if it seems so to the naked eye. Sitting on my bed at noon is a different environment (space) than sitting on my bed at 1pm because the lighting is different at 1:00 compared to noon. Maybe a dog is barking now, but wasn't barking at noon; thus, what I'm sensing and experiencing is again altered.

The light reflecting off the moon and Venus is slightly different, the traffic noise in the background has picked up, the gravitational pull coming from the Earth's core has adjusted slightly due to the Earth's rotation, and the smell of lunch foods being cooked at the neighbor's house has subsided. The list goes on, but the point is, there is no "same" environment or experience in life. Experiences are always changing and, as a result of consistent change, we, humans, are always growing.

In this case, You_x is the actuality of who you are — in totality — both known and unknown. Meaning, you are a different person in this moment than you were an hour ago. Your shape, perceptions, and thinking are constantly changing and adjusting based on your experiences.

So our growth formula would be written as:

$$Growth = (You_2 - You_1)/You_1$$

Where You_x is derived from the above formula and solved for as follows:

$$You_x = Experience_x/(Time \times Space)$$

It should be noted here that the primary growth we're talking about is in the areas of your mental and emotional expansion. The accumulation of life experiences will always contribute to an increase in your viability as a human and spiritual being regardless of your ability to take advantage and apply that experience. We as humans are dynamic, whether we're aware of and/or process the dynamism of our beings or not. When we can become aware of the changes we're gaining through experience and begin to note the idea that each experience is an opportunity to grow in some

emotional/spiritual way, we're utilizing the Progressive Love™ Tenet
— The Purpose is Growth.

When we can see each experience as having one sole purpose,
among the many specifics represented therein, we can definitely
state that the real underlying reason for experience itself has to
be growth.

The Benefit is Love

When it comes to relationships, the longer we stay together without
copping out or dropping out, or being in victim or villain mode,
or internalizing shame or passing on blame, the more we grow
inside of the relationship, the more the relationship blossoms and
we blossom as individuals. This is easier said than done because, in
our current relating culture, it's common to cop out of a relationship
and merely exist there for the sake of the kids, money, fear of being
alone and creating a new relationship, tradition, avoiding embarrassment from family, or whatever. We're also used to dropping
out or playing the blame game, thus, missing the opportunity to
gain the missing life skills that contributed to us being unhappy
in our relationships to begin with. The individuals who are able to
grow together inside of their relationship will see their relationship
grow as well. Isn't that the point of being in relationship? To grow
together? To become stronger individually and collectively? But
what's the benefit of becoming stronger? The answer is love. The
experience of the highest and purest forms of love on the planet.
Because nothing feels better than truly loving yourself and others,
especially when you've successfully navigated hardships together.

When I was in college, I pledged a fraternity with seven other
young men. It was a trying experience for all of us, to say the least.
We really hadn't been tested physically, emotionally, or mentally

like that before. Throughout the pledge process, we were forced to work together, support one another, and get past our insecurities. Not only were we forced to support each other, but we had to call each other out on our individual and collective bullshit. We had a number of fights throughout the ordeal, but we managed to get through it together. I can honestly say I've never felt a deeper love for anyone to that point in my life than I did for my line brothers. Every time I would see one of them on campus, I was instantly happy and felt full of love for them. It's a feeling that you would do anything for them. I still have that feeling for them to this day, over thirty years later.

But what is that love, really and practically? It's a feeling that I'll do anything I can to support them in their lives. It's the feeling that I'll give to them and I truly don't need anything in return from them. It's the desire to give to them because I'm able to do so. That's the feeling we're looking to generate in our relationships and marriages, but in order to get there, we must be willing to do the work.

What's interesting, though, is that one of my line brothers actually copped out of the process. He found a way to not participate with most of the pledge process, but still graduated with the rest of us. We actually fought for his graduation because we wanted him to be with us. However, I didn't have the same feeling for him as I did for my other brothers who went through the entire process together. It wasn't an intellectual or judgment thing; it just didn't feel the same. This is why we should never cop out of a relationship before the growth process can be fully experienced. It's just impossible to have a true, deep love for another person unless the two or more have grown together. I'm not saying we must do the work in one relationship without loving others, but it's different when we navigate troubled waters together and successful come out on the other side. Relationships are challenging to the point where we could say they're incubators for a larger growth process. Relationships are made to bring us closer together and find true love for all the beings we relate with. But we have to stay in the game and take responsibility for our lives. We have to go through real experiences together; otherwise, love is largely theoretical.

The more we go through as couples, friends, colleagues, family, the stronger we become and the more love and appreciation we have for one another, the more we realize that collective growth is one of the most powerful experiences on earth to bring human beings together in true love and intimacy. This is why it's worth it to not fall into victimhood in relationships and not assign the role of villain to others. This is why we need to not cop out of the relationship by not doing the work and withdrawing our emotional investment in our chosen relationships. The imperative growth process that love illuminates is why we shouldn't just drop out and leave before we're aware of the work. When we do these things, we deny the very gift each relationships can give. We are growing together and the fact we know this growth is challenging, for all involved should lead us to never feeling shame about our performance in the relationship and conversely assigning blame to others, based on our perceptions of their behavior. Love is about growth, all relationships that are growing will feel loving, and love is exactly what we want in our lives and relationships.

I Create My Life

The overall concept is that if I take total responsibility for my life then I have the power to create how it looks and appears to me. We take total responsibility by staying within the limits and confines of the Progressive Love™ tenets as listed above. This allows us to channel all of our available mental, emotional, and physical resources and abilities into creating what we want. Hopefully, that's fairly clear to everyone because the concept of total accountability isn't accepted in our society primarily because of the belief in chance, chaos, luck, karma, misfortune, and being in the wrong place at the wrong time. Meaning, our culture believes that certain aspects of life are random and separate from conscious and sub-conscious thought, in which case, it's impossible to create your life, right? Instead, you would simply do your best and hope nothing goes wrong in the process, even if we ignore the fact that we're at least partly hallucinating our lives and each person's hallucination is unique to them, their experiences, and personal stories. Most people believe there's only one reality that represents the absolute truth of the world and the only reason it may be perceived differently is because of our individual inability to align our sensory organs to accurately capture the details. This is essentially the error in thinking that prevents us from believing we have control over our lives — absolute reality, one truth, one perception, chaos, luck, karma, chance, etc.

We believe in those concepts as well except we believe they are mathematical in nature. For example, some have said luck equals preparation times opportunity. We would adjust that formula as such:

$$\text{LUCK} = (\text{Preparation} \times \text{Readiness in the Moment}) \times \text{Opportunity}$$

Opportunity, in this case, equals the correct moment in the time-space continuum that matches one's preparation to date.

Meaning, those who experience "good luck" were actually in a state of readiness and preparation and eventually hit a place in space and time where that readiness paid off (i.e., matched like two puzzle pieces). On the other hand, those who experienced "bad luck" weren't prepared and weren't ready for the moment at hand; thus, they experienced what we define as misfortune.

It can be said that chaos is simply someone being in a situation they're not prepared for and where they haven't accounted for all possible environmental forces at play. We know corporations spend billions of dollars to reduce chaos within factories and the workplace because it's costly and inefficient. They achieve this goal by injecting certainty into their work environments by implementing systems of consistency, control, tight management, and processing to catch errors and breakdowns. We can summarize this environment of certainty as order. Even in these environments, however, we find elements of chaos still exist, but (1) the extent of the damage caused by chaos is greatly limited by the controls put in place and (2) most competent executive teams will admit the probability of chaos was permissible only because of their conscious decision not to spend more capital on eliminating it. Meaning, finite resources play a part in a company's ability to implement safety protocols and control measures; however, the measure of potential chaos is evaluated as a necessary potential cost based on these budget restrictions. In other words, the chaos can be eliminated if the corporation had that goal in mind. We see this in the airline industry where airplane crashes must be avoided if these manufacturing companies wish to stay in business. However, larger levels of uncertainty are permissible in other transportation industries utilizing cars and trains because although lack of precision is costly, the perception of safety by its customer base and insurance companies is greater because it's ground travel. So, we see that chance, luck, and chaos have some level of controllability even for those who believe it's a constant.

The final element to observe in *I Create My Life* is the concept of Alignment. When we align our mental, emotional, and physical capabilities, we greatly reduce chaos and increase our chance of introducing certainty into our lives. Another way to state it is, if our mental focus is in line with our inner desire, we will move more expeditiously toward our goals and dreams. In addition, when our actions are also in alignment with our thoughts and emotions then we've achieved Alignment and maximized our ability to achieve the lives we desire. This is actually the true meaning of consciousness states like Zen or nirvana where the seamless integration of the physical (body and action), emotional (spirit), and mental (consciousness) is achieved. The only difference here is Alignment refers to Zen in motion, meaning that we don't have to sit in a state of meditation in a corner but, rather, live our authentic life that's totally aligned with our purpose. This is essentially Parabrahm Sarvikalpa Nirvana.

ALIGNMENT

Thus, our ability to create our lives is a function of our ability to achieve Alignment. This can be represented as follows:

$$Y = f(x)$$

where Y is the Creation of our Lives and $f(x)$ represents the function of the cumulative alignment of our mental, emotional, and physical selves as human beings; thus $f(x) = f(M, E, P)$, where M equals our mental focus and alignment, E equals our emotional state and direction, and P equals or physical state and actions of doing.

$$\text{Life Creation} = f(M, E, P)$$

When we say physical resources, we're actually referring to what we choose to actually do day-by-day, moment-by-moment. Meaning, where we are putting our physical efforts and whether those efforts are in alignment with where we are emotionally. A good example of misalignment is when we're working at a job we hate. Mentally, we think we need to work this job to pay the bills; however, our heart (i.e., emotions) are not into the job or the kind of work we're doing. Despite our emotions being out of alignment with our thinking, we drag ourselves into work every day anyway. This is the perfect example of a physical misalignment with our emotional and mental state. This translates into poor health, poor job performance, and a bad attitude on the job itself. When we look at the opposite side of the equation, someone who loves (i.e., emotional) their job, believes (i.e., mental) it's the right thing for them to focus their time and energy on, and goes (i.e., physical) to work every day as well as preparing their body (i.e., physical) for the task at hand, tends to have a better job performance and better health. These are often your Type A personality people who climb the corporate ladder rather quickly because they're clear on all levels. We can call this the achievement of Alignment.

MIS-ALIGNMENT

However, we don't want to paint of picture of success as Alignment because people often use their fear or pain as a driving force for achievement as well. Instead, what we're talking about here is something that generates the emotion of peace within, which is a manifestation of being sure and clear about one's life. That's the ultimate goal for good health, optimal mental performance, and the expeditious achievement of one's goals.

Many will say Nirvana is a state that's achieved by those on a spiritual path, but we would argue that it's a natural state for human beings once we're initiated out of our fears, conditionings, and dependency on our fight-or-flight responses as a means of our daily living. Achieving Alignment is what allows us to Create Our Lives because it trains our subconscious minds to support the lives we desire while simultaneously keeping all aspects of our being in alignment.

Duality of Being: Ego and Higher Self

We've discussed the *Progressive Love™ Philosophy* and tenets to give us a new perspective on how to view our lives. The goal of this philosophy is to seat us, firmly, in the driver's seat as creators of our lives. It's the key to personal empowerment and represents the highest level of personal accountability that exists on the planet. It's a great start to lay the groundwork for how we communicate with one another, especially loved ones. However, we need to understand a bit more about who we actually are because an objective look at our lives, choices, and behavior might show us we're *not* the masters of ourselves — mind, spirit, and body. One may even say, we're not the masters of our choices and ability to "will" our lives — which would make living the above Progressive Love™ Tenets impossible.

Part of us claims to want greatness, but another part of us chooses mediocrity or the easiest path. A part of us understands we should save money, work consistently, exercise, eat right, speak positively, be disciplined, read, pursue education, and avoid behaviors that are reckless and self-destructive, but another part of us leads us down alternative paths at every turn. This apparent dichotomy is so pervasive in our lives that we don't even think about it. We simply take for granted that what we say and what we do will often be two different realities because the part of us that "says" isn't always the part of us that "does" and to make things even more complex, the more we try to change patterns and habits, the less aligned the voices inside our head actually are. In other words, the saying and doing voices are certainly aligned when it comes to maintaining the status quo or doing what we've always done.

We need to make some sense of who we are so that we can begin the process of mastering self, achieving greatness, and communicating effectively with others, but first comes the acknowledgment and understanding of a truth — we are, at minimum, composed of two decision-making consciousnesses, with each having very different agendas and functions in our lives. Additionally, these two minds, so to speak, are imperceptible without practice, discipline, and self-awareness. They are hard to differentiate from one another; thus, making them difficult to manage. In truth, there are even more consciousnesses at play, but for the sake of this introduction, we'll keep it simple and focus on the duality. For now, let's call these two parts of the self *Ego and Higher Self.*

Let's give some context before going further into the technical details. My marriage with the co-author of this book, Kenya K. Stevens, was tumultuous at times to say the least. We both had intense personalities, were skilled verbally in arguments and debates, and reveled in the opportunity to draw lines in the sand and hold our ground. We brought those qualities into our marriage. When we went to counsel about our relationship early one Saturday morning, the spiritual advisors welcomed us. We wanted to know what the cards predicted about the quality of our union and future marriage. She shuffled the cards, spread them, and drew two cards. The first was Ausar Tu Tchaas and the second was Tehuti Hetep. These Kemetic archetypes were the two highest on the Tree of Life and were, therefore, linked to the *Higher Self*. She looked at us with some surprise and stated that our union was one of a very high order. "You both are here to do great life and spiritual work together this lifetime; however, this union will only last by you both observing your highest level of spiritual development and commitment." What she was essentially saying was we absolutely could not be in our Egos during the marriage and hope to survive.

Of course, we left that consultation feeling great about the prognosis for our relationship, but, in truth, not really understanding what we had just been told. We really had no idea what the *Higher Self* even was or what it looked like in action daily. To further complicate things, our definition of *Ego* wasn't very sophisticated either. In our minds, the Ego was just a reflection of sometimes having an attitude when we wanted to get our way, but outside of that, we never really considered it as important or relevant. Little did we know how accurate that assessment would be for our relationship.

In the years that followed, two things became apparent: (a) Kenya and I handled our emotions differently and (b) we had different perspectives and interpretations of seemingly the same reality. She grew up in a household where emotions were expressed via rage and violence whether verbally or physically. Another way to state it is that force was her primary method of dealing with emotion. My household was the polar opposite because, although emotions ran high, everything was held in. My mother and father divorced when I was eight years old and only during these types of life-changing events did I get to see any kind of real emotion on display. When my mother came home and collapsed on the floor crying because she saw my father at a restaurant with another woman instead of studying for his graduate work, it was the ultimate display of internalization of emotions. She didn't make a scene at the restaurant. No flipping tables or screaming, "Who's this b****?!" Even when he came home, she didn't lash out or attack him but, instead, cried uncontrollably. One might say this is a display of power, in which energy is gathered and harnessed for its potential rather than immediate application. Powerful internalization of emotion is often seen as a more noble way to deal with the trials of life because they don't directly infringe upon others, but that's just an illusion.

So, when Kenya and I would attempt to communicate, she would utilize the force she had learned to get her expression out of her body, while I utilized a more internal or even passive aggressive display. Rarely would I allow strong emotion out, which also held back passion and joy to some extent. Kenya was livid when I wouldn't come forward with how I felt. I was annoyed when Kenya would forcefully express her emotion. All in all, we were BOTH utilizing the Ego and didn't know it. What's worse is we were utilizing the Ego as a primary way to communicate in our relationship, albeit I felt she was the one in Ego due to use of force. I had no idea then that I too was in Ego as I held in my feelings, thoughts, and emotions.

Most of us can only hold in so much when it comes to our feelings. At some point, we need to let it out. We need an exhaust system; otherwise, we can expect an explosion at some point or even worse, an irreversible damaging of the system attempting to control the energy, which, in this case, is our physical bodies. In other words, we can get sick because energy was never meant to sit still. Mentally, we can build up a permanent resentment toward loved ones and life because the energy has literally shaped our thinking. By its very nature, energy moves through any channel available to it, and when a channel isn't available, it challenges the structural integrity of the boundaries attempting to hold it in.

So, the variance between the way I had learned to process emotion, internally, and the way Kenya processed emotion, forcefully and externally, became the challenge our Egos would face. Fortunately, we had become aware of one of the principles of the Progressive Love™ Tenets very early in our marriage — *The Purpose is Growth*. So instead of allowing our emotional incongruence to derail our relationship, we set off to explore the variance and find harmony there. Currently, we are well aware of the Duality within us, the Ego and the Higher Self. Each of these internal stations have given emotional expressions. We have fully embraced the influence of each.

Emotions are simply energy. They are feelings, because we can physically feel emotional energy moving throughout our body in various ways. What makes feelings or emotions, such as joy or pain, different or unique are the specific channels through which the energy travels. In other words, the feeling of joy is simply energy moving through a series of channels that we identify as joyful while sadness is energy moving through bodily channels we consider uncomfortable. Force is one lever used to release emotional energy traveling inside the body to channels leading it outside of the body. Power is a lever used to keep energy circulating through channels inside the body in such a way that the energy maintains its properties, but doesn't cause discomfort beyond what can be tolerated. Both force and power are utilized by the Ego to channel emotion!

So, up to this point, we have established two important pre-requisites to facilitating effective communication between people, especially those in relationships: (1) We have a dual consciousness existing within us that affects what emotions we generate and actively choose in life and (2) we carry and channel energy inside our bodies and these energies take the form of emotions. We are made of multiple, seemingly independent consciousnesses that choose, based on their individual purposes, how to channel energy (i.e., emotion) to carry out dualistic choices.

So, more about this duality of consciousness, as you now know, these consciousnesses can be categorized as the Higher Self and Ego. What differentiates them? The Higher Self is interested in bringing things and people together for the greater good of the whole. It wants experience for experience sake and houses the awareness of our omnipresence with all things, our omniscience of life, and our omnipotence and ability to accomplish anything we desire. We could say the Higher Self aligns with our cerebral cortex and higher brain functions as human beings. The Ego desires to substantiate its place and purpose in the world and does this through obtaining credit, having witnesses to its actions and accomplishments, and being the center of attention.

That makes it simple enough, right? If a choice benefits me first and only me, then it's one hundred percent the Ego, but if that choice benefits all involved in a balanced way, not necessarily equally, then it's the Higher Self. If I've acted without thought or rationality, primarily based on a fight or flight response mechanism, or based on what feels good, then that's the Ego. If I've acted with regard for the whole and knowing that all is here to grow me, the consciousness in motion is the Higher Self.

This gives us a great initial separation of our two inner aspects and a good starting point to analyze some of our past choices to see who was talking. But before we go there, let's eliminate the first temptation, which is to place one of these inner aspects above the other. The Higher Self isn't greater or better than the Ego. Both of our Aspects are necessary and play vital roles in our lives. Without the Ego, there's really no purpose for being here. Individuality is beautiful and provides us with amazing experiences and motivations for our lives. In and of itself, Ego isn't the bad guy, even though certain teachers will make that claim. From that same perspective, achieving the Higher Self level of consciousness isn't the ultimate goal of life when we leave the Ego behind and ascend into the clouds and live our lives out in the heavens. The Higher Self is simply a critical aspect of ourselves that keeps our lives in order and creates a healthy space for others to be present with us. We have to note that the Ego wishes to create a hierarchy and level of importance so that it can attain to something greater and then be recognized for that accomplishment. It's also the part of us that wants to use hierarchy as a reason why it may not have achieved its potential. The Ego needs reasons for failure or lack of achievement; thus, it spends much of its time segregating the world into categories then subsequently ranking them.

If we take some time to review our feelings over the years, we'll see that a part of us genuinely wants the best for others, including those we don't know. It's hard for most people to watch others being hurt or abused, unless we can somehow give ourselves a reason for that abuse. Without a reason, though, it never really *feels good* to watch any living being be harmed. This feeling of love and compassion and wanting the best for others is the Higher Self aspect of us. It's the part of us that feels their pain as they go through it in the same way that we feel happiness at their triumphs in life. A part of us wants everyone to be happy and to win at life. That's the

Higher Self in action. That part of us that wants to connect with and love others, just because, is the Higher Self.

Conversely, the part of us that feels fear around others doing well because they'll be recognized but we won't be is the Ego. It's not that we don't want others to succeed, but we don't want to be considered less than others or go unrecognized for our specialness. For that reason, the Ego pushes us and drives us forward to achieve and be recognized. It has us be unique and attempt to stand out and be witnessed by a group of our peers. Or maybe it pushes us to be famous so that we can have the ultimate witnessing by others. Whenever we see ourselves being fine with others experiencing pain, it's often because our Ego has passed judgment on that person or given them a label that puts them below us in some way. It revels in the fact that we're not them and are, therefore, better. We see the Ego at play with some married people who look down on those who are single or divorced. It's a ranking activity that it practices consistently to put itself at the top. Again, it's not a bad thing in and of itself, but we can certainly see how it can be destructive, especially when fear and other emotions are the driving force.

Sometimes, we see one group of people hurting another group, but we don't say anything because we're in fear of being grouped with the castigated group and looked down upon or even hurt ourselves. That's all Ego. The Higher Self is willing to act for the sake of the greater good even with the potential of personal loss or pain because its ultimate goal is unity and integration with the greater good. Does this mean the Higher Self gives away all its money so that everyone has the same amount? No because the Higher Self isn't about sameness, but equality. Just like the Higher Self is fine with the heart having access to more blood than the kidneys it would also be fine with the caretakers of wealth and material resources having more than those who don't value them. Equality and sameness are not the same thing. The same spiritual laws and being that gave us the Higher Self also gave us the Ego; thus, the variety of uniquenesses that we see present in every aspect of life, needs to be honored as well.

UPLVL Communication™: A New Way To Use Language

Given the specific nature of the Progressive Love™ Tenets, they become the prerequisite by which we build out an entirely new way to use language. After all, language gives us the old paradigm structure — to shame and blame others, or to twist someone into victim or villain. Language affects how we describe the events in our lives; and the way we describe events determines our perspective on events, which also determines whether we'll stay and work through challenges or cop out and drop out, running from *problems*. UPLVL Communication™ has, at its core, the Progressive Love™ Tenets and represents the needed shift in language to communicate in accordance with principles we value. If we value speaking to young people, loved ones, and friends with an eye toward taking a progressive approach, we must analyze and then rearrange the way we use language.

In order to set a stage for what in our language must change to accommodate a progressive view of self and others, we'll briefly explore the history of the English language.

Who Is Speaking?

Two of our most important tasks in establishing effective communication via the UPLVL Communication™ system are: (a) establishing who is speaking — Ego or Higher Self — and (b) giving both internal voices a space to speak and be heard. Doing this guarantees clarity and balance in our communications.

Establishing who is speaking when we communicate should be an easy task, given the expansive differences between the two possible voices — the Ego and the Higher Self. When my Ego is speaking, I have an acute focus on I, my, mine, how I feel, what I think, what my opinions are, and how I want things to be. Ego has a tendency to see *us vs. them* or *me vs. you* as a standard, segregating and categorizing things and beings into *right and wrong, good or bad.* Ego also has the tendency to alienate people and separate information into bits that classify and assign judgement in various situations. Ego also believes his or her perspective is the truth or the actual facts of any given matter — so it defines things — even when the definition may not match the reality. Keep in mind, there's nothing wrong with the Ego's perspective on life. It simply must be noted what the Ego's voice IS, what it says, and its intention.

The Higher Self, on the other hand, tends to speak in generalizations around how everything is good, and how everything serves to further our growth. You may have heard your own Higher Self tell you that "everything happens for a reason." This is a cliché example of the general tone of the Higher Self. It's the voice that says "everything will be alright" and it's very soothing when inserted in the right moments. The voice of the Higher Self might tend more toward presence, compassion, empathy, healing, and unity. This isn't to denote superiority of the Higher Self, but simply to define the style and thrust of the dual voices that humans house. In defining these, we can begin to answer the question of *who is speaking*, which will essentially open us to deeper levels of authentic communication.

Modern English language doesn't pose the question of who is speaking but rather who is being spoken about. Moreover, it asks whose voice are we hearing when an author writes — first person, second person, and so on. We concern ourselves with present or past tense, even future tense. But never do we ask ourselves which part of the author's consciousness is speaking. This is one of the areas where UPLVL Communication™ carves a new course for language itself. Which is mandatory if we would begin to utilize language to create deeper authenticity.

The History of the English Language

The English language was developed from a combination of Celtic languages native to England and emerging Germanic languages in the 5th century AD, and has gone through many changes since. In 1066 the developing English language was completely replaced by that of Nordic origin as the throne was brutally captured by Nordic and Germanic invaders. The war-torn environment present in the conception of the English language is worth noting only to demonstrate language itself is dynamic and can be utilized as an indicator to the emotional tone of culture. It is imperative to note the history of the English Language and how it originates, and the experience of the humans who created it. It is clear via linguistics specialists that emotion is transferred and constantly affected by a culture's language.

> An emotional version of Sapir–Whorf hypothesis suggests that differences in language emotionalities influence differences among cultures no less than conceptual differences. (Leonid Perlovsky, *Language and Emotion*)

If we apply an emotional study of the development of the English Language, we can easily see that the social systems arising where English is the primary language can be classified as *cultures of war,* because the language itself arose from various cultural groups warring and thus integrating and formulating language over the course of 1066 to present day. Only by the 17th century did the English language become a worldwide standard via imperialism, conquest, and tyranny. Thus, we consider the English language to be a *language of war.* It displaced most of the Celtic languages that had predominated England prior — Celtic cultures tended toward peace and nature alignment, while Germanic cultures thrived through conquering and waging war. The numerous wars that ensued as England settled into prominence shaped the language and all those who spoke it. And of course, we don't judge war as a negative; what we mean in noting the origins of the English language is to show the emotional atmosphere that might shape a few of its components; shaping factors that keep our modern conversational style in debate, contrast, argument, and comparison modalities, with few points of unification or empathy.

To simplify, the English language is based on "othering" rather than unifying. We can see this in how we conjugate verbs. This is seen most clearly in the conjugation of the verb *to be* as a means to support the clear differentiation of the person speaking or being referred too. The verbs *am, are,* and *is* support the denotation and separation of specific sets of individuals. In this case, *am* is used to assign the action to the single individual speaking in the present tense. For example, "I am happy." Who's happy? Me. When is the happiness being experienced? Right now, in the present. This seems so simple and we're all quite used to speaking and writing in this way, but we must recognize the natural separation from all other things, including God, spirit, or any other human aspect that could possibly unify us in some way. If we don't specifically use the *are* to denote a collective, we find separation is implicit. For example, "We are happy." In this instance, we experience some inclusion with others, but exclusion is still implicit. The statement "We are happy," could be referring to only two individuals out of forty in a room. Unless we add determining words like *all* or *people* to the sentence, the separation will continue to be implicit. For example, "We are all happy" or "All people are happy." The point of the exercise is to note the subtle work required to unify and include and the ease in separating simply based on the structure of the English language. This subtlety absolutely affects how we interact and relate with one another. It affects how we view one another because our language is naturally divisive.

The English language supports six different person references, all designed to provide clear separation – first person singular, second person singular, third person singular, first person plural, second person plural, and third person plural. In other words, English has six different ways to separate the subject (i.e., the person or people being referenced) from others. Again, not only are people separated but also moments in time, which further disconnects us from each other. Are we saying this is a bad thing? Of course not; however, the fact there is no natural and seamless alternative that's inclusive of all things is problematic in our ability to unify with each other. In other words, how can we feel a natural connection and closeness with all other humans if we have no language for it? How can we feel close to our wives, girlfriends, husbands, and boyfriends if our language is subtly yet explicitly separating us from one another? What's the conjugated form of the verb *to be* for the all and everything? We only have it partially for the first person plural, as in "We are happy."

We see the same separation with the use of pronouns in the English language as well such as *I, You, We, Mine, Yours, Ours, Them,* and *Us.* The latest movement in this country is over the use of pronouns and the battle to get out of the binary gender box of male and female. What's not recognized by those inside the non-binary movement; however, is that the battle is inside of the language itself and not towards the people using the language. It's the English language that promotes separation and specific categorization with no means of escape. Why is this a problem? Because with categorization comes labeling, and with labeling comes presumption of one's being, skill, ability, and preference, which are things that have profound impacts on us socially and economically. What we identify as could prevent us from being chosen on a dating application or from being admitted into certain job positions. It gets deep.

But let's not forget the focus of our work here – improving the communication effectiveness in our relationships such that we clearly hear one another and move from a language of war into a language of love. In the business environment, they say there's no "I" in TEAM. The implication is that when one focuses on themselves too intently, it takes away from the effectiveness of the team as a whole. Well, the same applies in relationships too. There's no "I" in US, but when you listen to people talking to one another inside of relationships, we hear a lot of "I," "Me," "You," "Mine," "Yours," etc. and not enough "We" and "Us." The more we use "I," the farther apart we become.

The English language creates terms like *mine, yours, ours, his, theirs,* and *hers,* where other languages may not have words that depict individual ownership, thus creating less to war about in such cultures. For example, the Dogon culture of central, west Africa has a language wherein verbs are conjugated differently. The Mali Empire where the Dogon people originated held prominence from 1230 to 1610. The empire was founded by Sundiata Keita, and became renowned for the wealth of its rulers, especially Mansa Musa. For the Dogon culture, Amma (a female goddess) created the Earth. But Amma forgot to bring unity and thus nothing in the world worked. So Amma began again, this time, weaving unity into creation.

Dogon language was created around an intentional nod to unity and the necessity of both aspects of human life — the Ego and the Higher Self. It's verbs are conjugated differently from English verbs and Dogon language includes a stop gap measure to incorporate the divine aspect of all things into verbs and nouns. English conjugates it's pronouns and nouns to make everything appear separate: *she, him, her, they, us, them, me, I,* and *mine.* Bantu language includes *tu* in all words denoting nouns (persons places or things) and has no pronouns. For example, *muntu* (a bantu person), *kintu* (an impersonal force), *hantu* (position in time) and *kuntu* (a way of being), all include the word *tu,* which literally means 'the divine or God/Goddess.' Tu is the cord that ties humans, plants, animals, positions in time, and objects together. *Bantu,* for instance, means all humans (past, present and future existing) and the *tu* means all humans are essentially divine.

There are many other indigenous languages to explore that weave the divine nature of humans (higher self) with the base nature (ego). The Sanskrit word, *namaste* is one. It literally translates to 'I bow to the divine nature in you.' This denotes the dual nature of humans, both the divine aspect (Higher Self) and the human (Ego). In this way, the cultures that utilize more wholistic languages have a different emotional demeanor than cultures whose language separates humans, excludes our divinity, and focuses on the Ego alone. And we can with the English language or any language create these kinds of usage shifts in order to bring holistic understanding and connected communication through.

What UPLVL Communication™ will do is introduce a way to upgrade our language by adding nuances that denote who is speaking, as well as take out the warring facet of our cultural paradigm as expressed through conversation style and language use. We'll do that by interrupting the typical dance of language — analysis, interrogation, singling out, and pointing fingers — and rearrange our word use to create an authentic way to communicate that always references which part of the consciousness is speaking. Once this is complete, we'll essentially utilize language in a more empathetic way, which, I suppose, is the creation of a new language via use. It takes practice to come out of one paradigm and into another. Language and the examination of how it's used, moreover, shifting how it's used, is a step out of a warring paradigm that keep us stuck in Ego, othering, and even self-aggregation.

Part 2 — The Four Gateways

Next, we'll explore the four gateways of the UPLVL Communication™ system. The flow of the gateways are chronological and flow in a specific order.

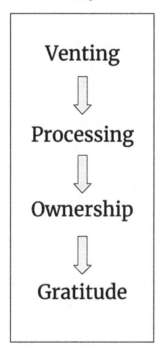

UPLVL
Communication™
Gateway Flow

Venting

⬇

Processing

⬇

Ownership

⬇

Gratitude

Gateway #1 — VENTING

"I shall look at you out of the corner of my eye, and you will say nothing. Words are the source of misunderstandings."

~ Antoine de Saint-Exupéry

Ego & the Animal

Coming to grips with our nature is one of the most critical aspects of our self-awareness journey. Many of us get caught up in the bright lights of human accomplishment and use it as a means to separate ourselves from who we are — *animals*. It can be a tough pill to swallow, but it's true. Is being an animal a problem? It is when we're in denial of that fact and, thus, allow the animal to consume our lives through addiction, lack of discipline, anxiety, and sharp fluctuations in emotional intelligence. Living unaware or in denial of the Animal portion of human nature is why happiness seems to elude us throughout most of our lifetimes. Or even worse, when we judge what it means to be an animal as something ugly, grotesque, simplistic, unintelligent, and barbaric instead of cute, compassionate, and cuddly; we loathe ourselves as the multifaceted beings we are. Outside of denial and judgment, there's absolutely nothing wrong with being animals. Welcome to your real life. When we embrace our Animal nature, we can discuss what the Animal within us needs and wants. We can even get into the purpose of the Animal within and, most importantly, HOW exactly the Animal within us communicates.

The Animal is here to protect us and keep us safe from harm using the oldest parts of our nature as tools to do so — the animated aspect to our self-preservation program. That's all the

Animal knows, really: protect, destroy or run from threats, run from pain, seek comfort and pleasure, secure sustenance, reproduce, and survive. I know it sounds a bit archaic and uncivilized, but it's supposed to sound that way because the Animal isn't civilized in the least and doesn't care to be. Ever further, we shouldn't want it to be civilized because most of our actual lives take place outside of our idea of civilization. The oldest part of who we are isn't civilized but reflexive and instinctual. It moves based on feelings, instinct, and a drive to survive. We could say the Animal aligns with the heart and emotions of human beings and is interested in survival, avoiding pain, seeking pleasure, and perpetuating itself through sex at any and all costs. It operates primarily based on how it feels via its five senses.

The Animal doesn't care about human advancement or invention; although, it would love to use those things to accomplish its primary tasks in life. The Animal doesn't care about education, graduation, career, family, community, the sanctity of marriage, money, etiquette, courtesy, or political correctness. It doesn't care what side of the plate the knife, fork, and spoon are placed. But this is where we need to be careful not to judge because everything has its purpose and function in our lives. We loathe the Animal in theory, but embrace it dearly when it saves our lives, gets us out of jam, or prevents us from being abused. We love the Animal's quick reflexes when we're driving and avoiding danger. We love it in sports when we're in need of that extra edge or burst to overpower or outlast our opponents. We love that Animal when it pushes us to defeat competition in the classroom or in business. We love the Animal for its passion during sex and love-making, especially when the connection is brand new. We love how it doesn't let us quit on life, but compels us to push onward and upward even through seemingly insurmountable pain and difficulty. The truth is, many of us would have checked out decades ago if it hadn't been for our inner Animal's desire for continued life. It believes in us, even when a part of us doesn't. It gets us through those challenges we never thought we could. So let's make no mistake about the importance of the Animal aspect of our being.

Take a moment to connect with your inner Animal. What kind of Animal is it? For some, it's the shy, timid, and playful kitten. For others, it may be the powerful, confident, and arrogant lion. Or maybe the sneaky snake, sexy cat, or social dog. Again, the Animal isn't bad. It just does what it does, which can either support us in our goals or get in the way. The important thing is getting to know our Animals personally and acknowledging their behaviors, habits, and tendencies so we don't get confused about who's actually speaking through us at various times of our lives. In addition, we need to understand how to allow our Animals to express themselves rather than hiding them away.

Thus far, we've covered three aspects of our make-up as human beings: Animal, Ego, and Higher Self, and, in so doing, we're simply stating that the human being is a complex, multifaceted organism with a variety of needs, inputs, and, yes, communication styles.

Is the Animal the Ego?

The Animal isn't the Ego. The Ego is the part of the mind that mediates between the conscious and the unconscious and is responsible for reality testing and a sense of personal identity. So, the Ego is a mediator; it's the mind's thinking position. It has the ability, unlike the Animal, to choose a position, in which the Animal has no choice; it functions from pure instinct and its position is based upon how it feels. Here's a great example: the Animal is enraged because her boss has just fired her for being late to work consecutively due to dealing with a sick child for weeks. Her Animal is fuming, bathing in fight or flight hormones, ready to kill someone! But the Ego, being the kind of mediator it is, has masked the Animal's anger, choosing, instead, to accept the firing as part of life and bid the boss a thank you for five years of employment. The Ego may let out a few words of the Animal's pure anger and demonstrate acceptable levels of disappointment via facial expressions, stomping, and shoving desk items into a box. But the overwhelming rage of the Animal remains seething beneath the surface.

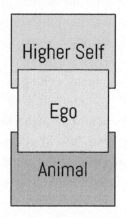

Later, at home, and in the presence of friends, the Ego chooses to allow more of the Animal's rage to surface from within, depending on how close the friends are. She now throws a visible tantrum, tossing her cup of tea across the room hitting the wall when she retells the story of her firing to close friends.

The Ego decides how the core instinctual reality of ourselves will be shown externally. The Ego mediates between the Animal within us and others. Ego is usually choosing actions based on societal norms and, thus, is trained and trainable. Ego is the gateway through which we can express our inner Animal or not.

When we choose to express the Animal, Ego has sanctioned it. Ego has made the choice. (And this is the same with our Higher Self, as Ego is the gateway through which Higher Self can actually have an external voice. We will explore this more in the section on Higher Self). So, Ego, in all its glory, isn't a negative aspect of the self; it's just a gatekeeper that holds self-interest at its core when trained by society to do so. Each culture trains the Ego differently, creating varied kinds of cultural paradigms. In fact, how we train the Ego to manage the Animal is what creates culture. For example, Inuit tribal communities historically trained youth to control impulse around anger, to express anger in productive ways, rather than suppress or act out. The tribal mothers in Inuit communities did this using storytelling as a way to express anger rather than punishments or time outs. Youth were given an opportunity to tell a story about how they felt when in the heat of anger as demonstrated by parents. Jean Briggs, a Harvard student, had the opportunity to study this culture in the late 1990s and noted, "They never acted in anger toward me, although they were angry with me an awful lot" (NPR News, Jane Greenhalgh).

What's important to note is Ego is trainable, Animal isn't so readily trainable, but it's possible to harness the Animal for various tasks and duties. The raw emotion of the Animal will never be fully undone, but it can be channeled. Culture is the vehicle for this training, and culture is the outcome of the training. Think of tigers trained in the circus. A cage is still around them; they've been trained to roll over at the sight of food or jump from this place to that, but we cannot fully undo their animal nature. The cage represents this. Ego and Animal are closely related, but they're not the same.

So, what are some examples of how the Animal may express itself in your life? For this, we look to the wisdom of the ancients. We'll find most African, Eastern, Native American, and South/Central American cultures used animals as totems to communicate how our inner Animal nature may express itself through us at any particular time. How did they know which animal was the dominant expression through a given individual? Observation, astrology, readings, or receiving messaging concerning the inherent nature of the child. We see this in Chinese astrology where each year is governed by a particular animal and whoever is born in that year will take on the characteristics of that animal.

Here are some animal expressions that we can use to assess ourselves and others.

- **Sloth** — The sloth is slow to move and spends most of its time eating, sleeping, and observing its environment. You could say they're laid back or even lazy, but definitely slow to move regardless of what the emergency may be. They appear to just be looking for peace and calm in their life. If you see yourself or others as being a bit stubborn and insistent on moving slowly and on their time, it may be their inner animal coming out in the form of the sloth. If you see someone being extra lazy and not wanting to put in the hard work, it may also align with the sloth.
- **Peacock** — The peacock loves to be seen, admired, and gushed over. It loves to stand out from everyone else and receive all the accolades. When the peacock functions through us, we also want to be recognized for our beauty, physique, dress,

our look, or an item that we possess like a new car or house. This is our inner peacock wanting to be seen.

- **Dolphin** — The dolphin is a communal and family oriented animal that is playful and likes to stick with the pack. They tend to be nice and nurturing to one another and other animals who aren't its prey. When you find yourself desiring family, community, safety, playfulness, and protection, it may be your inner dolphin Animal nature expressing itself.

- **Snake** — The snake is primarily to itself and uses its cunning to get what it wants. It's a slick creature who will strike you when you're not looking. It hides itself to conceal its whereabouts and intentions. Snakes can literally be anywhere and fit into any space without anyone knowing. When you see yourself being sneaky, cunning, and reacting based on vibrations and energy, you may be in your snake Animal nature.

- **Lion** — The lion is the ruler of its domain and carries itself in such a way that everyone knows it. They use the threat of speed, brute force, and teamwork to intimidate others in their environment. They can be both playful or cruel with one another and treat you largely based on how much you respect them. When you see yourself being confident, arrogant, imposing your will through the threat of force or violence, then you may be in your lion Animal nature.

- **Owl** — The owl is a nocturnal animal who hunts and feeds in the dark. It uses the dark to conceal itself and sleeps during the day. They have excellent eyesight and spend most of their time observing, studying, and mastering their environment. They can turn their heads and look behind them without moving their bodies, which potentially makes them wiser than most animals in the environment because less energy is required to observe and see everything. When you find yourself preferring to do things at night, hide your true nature, observe people and things rather than participate, and refrain from daily physical activities, you may be in your owl Animal nature.

- **Bull** — The bull is powerful and utilizes force to intimidate others and remove obstructions in its path. It prefers to be seen and isn't into niceties. It has a ravenous sexual appetite and high levels of testosterone. When you find yourself using force and intimidation as a tactic to influence your environment, you may be channeling your inner bull animal nature. In addition, when you find yourself making decisions based on your ravenous sexual appetite, you may also be channeling the bull Animal nature within you.

- **Gorilla** — The gorilla is a territorial animal that seeks dominion over all other animals within its environment. It spends a tremendous amount of time relaxing, sleeping, eating, and mating, but also desires to play or fight at times. They tend to have a short temper but can also be kind, playful, and inviting. Whenever you find yourself being territorial for the express purpose of relaxing, lounging, and being lazy, you may be in your gorilla Animal nature.

- **Dog** — The dog tends to be loyal, pack-oriented, cunning, and, at times, sneaky. Its time is spent seeking food. It has the ability to run fast, climb, dig, and outwit its enemies, which can make it quite dangerous. When you find yourself being loyal to get ahead in life or using your cunningness to get what you want, you may be in your dog Animal nature.

- **Cat** — The cat is finicky, playful, at times lazy, and carefree. Cats are also the best hunters on the planet because of their speed, quickness, and ability to be silent while moving. They have no loyalties and gravitate toward whatever makes them feel good in the moment. When you find yourself gravitating toward the comforts of the world, being indecisive, or being deceptively ruthless, you could be in your cat Animal nature.

These are just a few animal examples, but enough to give us a picture of the various ways the Animal may function within us. The Animal expression within human beings is never linear, but instead rather varied and complex. In addition, we each tend to gravitate toward certain Animal expressions at different times of our lives and in specific situations.

The Higher Self, Ego, & Animal in Summary

Here is a summary of these aspects of the human makeup.

Higher Self — that part of us that is connected to our ability to identify with all other beings in the world and recognize our common consciousness and source of being. Also, our ability to know and understand the underlying forces, cycles, energy, and order that governs our life and the world in general. The Higher Self possesses our ability to achieve all things through our innate creative power. It's interested in guaranteeing our individual existence and life experiences while simultaneously guaranteeing the life and experiences of all others. It's that part of us that's tapped into the laws that govern all of existence and thus gravitates toward unifying everything in the world to have its unique expression.

Ego — that part of us that desires to be recognized as unique and different from all other beings. The Ego holds our individual desired identity. The Ego has access to both the Higher Self and the Animal and serves as an intermediary between the two by expressing each one as the situation demands. The Ego is our personal mechanism responsible for choosing our path and evaluates reality in order to understand how to relate to it. The Ego is the part of us that establishes laws and order in our lives. It attempts to mimic the order implicit to the Higher Self in so doing, but often creates laws that uplift itself at the expense of others. The Ego's strength and weakness is its desire and ability to rationalize and interpret its reality (i.e., thinking).

Animal — that part of us that reacts to life based on feeling. Our inner Animal nature is driven by basic needs, wants, and stimuli coming from the environment. It isn't interested in how it's perceived by others, but in its level of comfort and safety. The Animal is primarily driven by emotional responses and reactions and uses memory as its primary reference point for interpreting its environment. The Animal tends to operate in the short term only and isn't interested in rules or order; however, its life, when not triggered, operates within the order established by the Higher Self.

> *"Loneliness does not come from having no people about one, but from being unable to communicate the things that seem important to oneself, or from holding certain views which others find inadmissible."*
>
> ~ Carl Gustav Jung

Why Venting is Mandatory

Venting is the language of the Animal, except animals don't utilize language that humans can discern, readily; so, venting then, is the language of the Animal, expressed through the Ego. Ego translates our Animal's feelings, words, and moods, and expresses whatever our Animal is sensing, where appropriate. Venting, however, is usually not appropriate. In fact, venting, the expression of raw emotion from deep within ourselves, is usually not embraced past infancy. Babies are allowed to vent. Babies can cry all day long because it's known their Ego isn't yet developed to the point where parents can hold them accountable for their actions thus, their dissatisfaction with the Animal expressions (crying, cooing, whining, etc.) are noted and integrated. Babies are solely in their Animal nature when they cry out in the night, no matter the time, or when they vent about being hungry, afraid, or lonely. Venting is about expressing a primal need, desire, pain, or joy.

Only after several years of being born, the Ego develops and takes its seat as mediator of the Animal, deciding what the Animal will be allowed to express externally! Tantrums and fits — both considered venting — then become less frequent in children whose parents have trained the Ego to curtail those behaviors. Venting is seen as immature and less desirable in older youth, even to the point of suppressing our basic human needs to not be viewed as inappropriate. However, our Animal nature still becomes emotive when we go through situations that we love, hate, desire, or abhor. We adjust to curtailing the Animal and silence it when Ego knows we might get into trouble if we share. This begins the lack of authentic communication. This, seemingly mandatory, culturally based suppression of our Animal instincts and feelings without space to vent them fully becomes the mask we wear that thwarts communication.

UPLVL Communication™ begins to unravel this systemic, cultural concern with the concept of Venting. Venting becomes mandatory in this system and the faster we learn to Vent inside a safe container, which we'll discuss, the more richly we become reconnected to everyone around us. Venting in a safe container is a simple concept. Think of an animal like a tiger or snake. Would we allow these kinds of animals to freely roam in our homes and offices? I'm not sure many would. So, when we consider the concept of introducing our Animal natures back into civilized areas, we must contain the Animal — not to suppress its expression, but to ensure no one is injured by our Animals.

Western culture has attempted to ensure no one is hurt by our inner Animals by creating rules, laws, norms, and standards that actually hide or degrade the Animal — Christian sin is such a concept. Sin means there are things we shouldn't do, lest we be considered adversaries of God. For those practicing the Christian faith, murder, adultery, and stealing are seen as sins. What we fail to realize is these actions are instinctual at times, and animalistic. Murder is an animal instinct humans can draw upon when in literal danger. Adultery is an animal instinct women possess, based on scent and the instinctual drive to reproduce via the scent of a man that best denotes powerful DNA for reproduction, without regard for human laws and marital structure. Stealing is a survival tactic from our Animal nature... and so on. The point is, our Animals are shut away via concepts that don't allow them safe space to exist, but the Animal cannot be silenced, if a culture doesn't recognize the vital importance of the Animal nature, and attempts to shut it away, the powerful, natural force of Animal energy will surface elsewhere, in the cracks and crevices between the rules; inducing perversions, hidden motives, and the evils of racism, sexism, and other isms.

The psychological ramifications of us attempting to beat the Animal away from ourselves is the crux of the communication issues of our time and the Ego is the main accomplice, by no fault of its own, of course. Again, Ego is trainable. It is precisely Ego who is trained in elementary schools to sit still, stop crying, stop day-dreaming, and communicate only when spoken to or after raising a hand. And since Ego is the mediator or mouthpiece for Animal, our Animal must sit and wait to express itself. Usually, there is no appropriate time given for the Animal to express, except maybe recess, but the regulations continue. With continued regulations and enforcements that the Animal nature in us is inappropriate, we become used to pinching off communication, choosing our words carefully, and walking on eggshells everywhere in civilized life. So, opening this inner world back up to the public in a contained manner becomes imperative for aligning ourselves internally with our external world. Venting is the first step on that journey.

Venting not only allows us to be more authentic in our communication and actually connect vulnerably to others, but it opens a doorway for actual release of emotions many scientists now associate with illness and even early death.

A series of studies over the past few decades show that suppressing your emotions can and does affect your body and your mind. In fact, a 2013 study by the Harvard School of Public Health and the University of Rochester showed people who bottled up their emotions increased their chance of premature death from all causes by more than 30%, with their risk of being diagnosed with cancer increasing by 70%. (Lucy E Cousins. https://www.hcf. com.au/health-agenda/body-mind/mental-health/downsides-to-always-being-positive)

So, venting becomes mandatory not just to improve our overall communication style, but to save lives! Once we discover the power of venting, we'll see why its step one on our UPLVL Communication™ journey, and mandatory for any communication to be viable between coworkers, families, and lovers. It is the number one most vital thing we can do in order to love ourselves and others. Once we're used to allowing Animal to speak via Ego in a container that makes everyone involved safe, we will have created a new kind of culture wherein there is total alignment between all facets of our inner world that connect deeply to the world without.

Venting Steps Summarized

Here are the step-by-step instructions for how to do a vent.

Venting Flow Chart

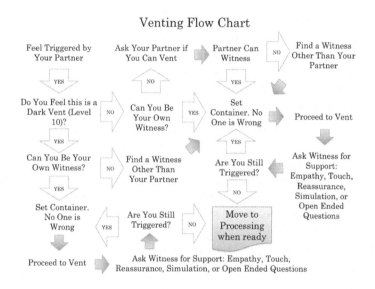

Venting Steps
Step 1: Are you triggered by what someone said, did, or by an event? If YES, go to Step 2. If NO, there's no need to vent at this time.
Step 2: Do you feel like this is a Dark Vent (i.e., Level 10 out of 10)? If YES, keep in mind that you may not be able to be your own Witness during your vent, so answer honestly to yourself in Step 3.
Step 3: Can you (or would you like to) be your own Witness; meaning, can you vent to yourself? If NO (i.e., Dark Vent, etc.) go to Step 4. If YES go to Step 6.
Step 4: Find a Witness to hear your vent. **NOTE:** The Witness might not be the person who triggered you, and that's okay and sometimes preferable.

Step 5: Set container.
Step 6: Proceed to vent. Allow the emotions and truth of how your Ego and Animal feel to come out. Make a clear statement that you're done venting when finished, for example, "That's all I have to say about it. I'm done."
Step 7: Ask the Witness for support in the form of either empathy, touch, reassurance, a simulation, or ask open-ended questions. **NOTE**: The Witness can also initiate the question of how the person venting needs support, but if they don't ask, simply let them know how you'd like to be supported.
Step 8: Do you still have unanswered questions that you need to ask in order to feel heard? If YES, to go to Step 9. If NO, go to Step 10.
Step 9: Set Container again and ask open-ended questions. **NOTE**: This isn't a back and forth. Once the question is answered, say, "Thank you for answering," and move on to the next question if there are more to ask. **NOTE**: You may also have an Open-Ended Discussion at this point. See the section on the Pluralities in PART 3 for details.
Step 10: Ask yourself if you're still triggered. If YES, go to Step 5. If NO, move to Processing when you're ready.

Venting Steps in Detail

Let's go a little deeper into each of these steps.

How to Know if You're Triggered

For Step 1, how do we know if we need to vent? There are two ways to determine if we need to vent: (1) are we still alive and (2) have we been triggered by an event of some kind. If we're alive, we need to vent regularly, but the big question is when exactly should we vent. Again, venting is the equivalent of removing physical waste from the body via the defecation process. How do we know we need to physically defecate? We can feel it in our body. We feel pressure and the urge to do so. When it comes to venting, we're removing mental and emotional waste that is stored in the cells of the body, but manifests in our minds. We know that waste is there because we become emotional in a way that feels uncomfortable (i.e., sadness, anger, jealousy, anxiety, depression, envy, guilt, shame, etc.). In simpler terms, when we don't feel good emotionally, we most likely need to vent.

It's actually a practice improved over time, when it comes to knowing when to vent. Yes, sometimes, it's obvious that we're upset with our partners, boss, children, or our lives in general, but other times, we may not be in touch with our feelings. We may be fuming below the surface, but because we've been trained to suppress our emotions throughout our lives, we may not realize we're triggered. We've been told to "suck it up" so many times in our lives when it comes to going to a job we don't like, or being in an unsatisfactory marriage, or enduring family members that we've often lost touch with how we feel. So, yes, it can difficult for us to feel when we need to vent because we're not always in touch with our bodies.

In addition to not being in touch with our bodies, we need to deal with the fact that feeling strong emotions is physically painful to us; therefore, we develop the habit of suppressing our emotions in order to avoid feeling physical pain. For example, when we're watching a sad movie, we may hold back the tears because it makes us physically uncomfortable to cry uncontrollably for an extended period of time. It hurts the chest cavity and heart. Feeling anger can be painful in our shoulders, neck, and head. Depression can paralyze the entire body and cause discomfort in our back and abdomen, and so on. It's hard to feel what our Ego (based on conditioning) doesn't want to feel.

So, assessing our need to vent requires awareness of ourselves and our bodies and honesty. We need to be truthful with ourselves about how we feel and resist the temptation to live in denial or simply assume that things will get better with time. Denial is a challenge we all face at various points in our lives because we feel guilty about how we ended up where we don't want to be. We feel like failures or that we wasted our time or lives. It's okay to feel that way because it's a natural tendency, but we need to fight as hard as we can to not allow that denial to stop us from creating the lives we desire. Change is a constant and we will forever be making changes and shifts in our lives. That's just a fact. Having emotions is part of the dynamism of living.

Another way to assess if we need to vent is by observing where we are relative to the Progressive Love™ Tenets:

- No Shame, No Blame
- No Victims, No Villains
- No Cop Outs, No Drop Outs
- The Purpose is Growth
- The Benefit is Love

The tenets are a prerequisite for the UPLVL Communication™ system because they denote the actuality of the Higher Self within each of us. Anyone who believes they're within their Higher Self when they feel like the victim or want to blame others for their failures will never see they're being in their Animal or Ego consciousness. Usually, in Western culture, when we're blaming another person for our own misery, it's sanctioned and given credence. Conversely, the UPLVL Communication™ system gives us a benchmark for testing our emotions and thoughts, and an indicator of when we surely need to vent. Anytime we're having a thought that isn't aligned to the Progressive Love™ Tenets outlined above, we need to vent.

So, if we ever feel like we're victims in a given situation, we know we're going against the tenets of our Higher Selves, so we clearly need to vent. If we ever feel like we're the villain or that someone else is the victim in a situation, we need to vent. If we ever feel like we just want to leave a relationship due to feeling uncomfortable or unhappy, we probably need to vent. If we feel like we want to stay in a relationship or job, but we aren't going to give our best effort, we probably need to vent. If we feel shame for a behavior or choice that we've made then we need to vent. If we feel like we want to blame others for our lives or feelings, then we probably need to vent. If we feel like the purpose of our relationships is to bring us happiness or anything other than growth, but we're not seeing that happen, then we probably need to vent. If we don't see all the lessons, hardships, and challenges of life as a part of our lives supporting us in coming into a higher state of love, then we probably need to vent. If we don't feel like we have the power and ability to create our lives, then we probably need to vent. The Progressive Love™ Tenets do a great job of centering us inside of our Higher Self, so there's no doubt about where we are at any particular time in our lives. We know exactly who's experiencing and perceiving the events we encounter every day. If we're outside the tenets, then, most likely, we're in Animal or Ego. If we're inside of them, then we're most likely inside our Higher Selves.

A Vent Is Essentially a Lie

Keep in mind, before we go further into how to vent, that a vent is essentially a lie. Why? A vent is based on one's personal perspective. This is similar to the concept of objectivity versus subjectivity. It is subjective to say, for instance, that a person has *disrespected* us. In one sense, it might feel very real that a person who loudly burps after dinner is being disrespectful. However, in many parts of India, burping after dinner isn't seen as disrespectful in the least but actually complimentary. There are many such scenarios. In fact, everything we personally perceive is subjective in nature. An objective view would simply note that something has occurred. Something transpired. Something IS. A subjective view assesses blame, shame, categories, definitions, motives, and meanings to reality. It is within these subjective meanings, some call these stories, where we identify the lie.

When we say a vent is a lie, it doesn't mean the person isn't experiencing some pain or discomfort. We simply mean the venting party is experiencing his or her own perspective or story around what actually occurred, so for the purposes of UPLVL Communication™, which aligns us to the Progressive Love™ Tenets and thus our Higher Selves, we identify all personal perspectives as lies, fallacies of the Ego, and interpretations that separate us from the actual truth of a given scenario.

Dark Vents

What is a Dark Vent referred to in Step 2? All vents begin with feeling triggered. A trigger is any event that brings up emotion in us. It's one thing to say you're triggered, but it's another thing, entirely, to want to hurt someone or tear the building down as a result of being triggered. Sometimes, we go to a very dark place when we're triggered because an event has touched a deeply buried trauma within us. These traumas are often buried away so deeply in the subconscious mind that we forget they're there, until the trigger actually happens. In addition, certain behaviors and responses are considered socially unacceptable or could get us fired from our jobs or permanently, negatively labeled in society. Does it mean the feelings under these behaviors aren't justified? No, it doesn't, but remember that we live in a culture of behavior suppression, so only certain behaviors will be deemed acceptable.

Keep in mind, venting is the language of the wild, untamed Animal and the Animal doesn't have a place in civilized society because of the shame we feel for our Animal roots and our desire to maintain order. The triggered behaviors outside of public acceptance are what we call Dark Vents. Other vents may be harsh or full of negative expressions, but are considered within the limits of what society will accept as long as they aren't done too often. We expect people to get mad and fed up. We expect people to complain, tactfully, once and awhile. We even expect some physical confrontation from time to time, so it's not the vent itself that gets labeled a Dark Vent, but those that go beyond public acceptance. For example, a son may have a Dark Vent about his mother when he feels like he needs to call her certain expletives so his Animal can be heard. Generally, a person calling his mother any explicative is considered out of bounds.

The thing about Dark Vents is they can be highly triggering to the person witnessing the vent; therefore, extra care and consideration must be taken about whom we choose as a *Witness*. For example, it may be hard to vent to a boss or coworker if in the vent, we express they're incompetent and a low life. They may not be able to recover from that Animal-based criticism, even though it's established in the proper UPLVL Communication™ container. The container notes that everything being expressed is a *lie*, coming purely from Ego and Animal. Another thing about Dark Vents is they tend to be quite animated with a lot of emotional expression. Again, this is the Animal in full expression via the Ego, allowing itself to be heard and seen. These types of animated Dark Vents can be hard for the Witness and can challenge the integrity of the container they're trying to set on the venter's behalf. So, if the vent is a Dark Vent, it may be best to find someone to Witness other than the person who triggered you. This isn't a hard rule but should at least be considered.

Lastly, this is why it's important to carefully consider becoming a Witness of a Dark Vent as outlined in Step 3. This increases the likelihood of allowing the Animal to fully express itself without worrying about judgment from the Witness; however, it can be difficult to remain in your Higher Self as a Witness during a Dark Vent because of the likelihood of becoming triggered yourself. Nevertheless, it's a beautiful thing to give ourselves permission to fully express how we feel when we're either by ourselves or with others, namely a designated Witness because the more we do it, the more we open ourselves to feeling. Moreover, we become healthier due to explicitly releasing waste from the body via the Dark Vent.

Rating Your Vent

A Dark Vent is a level 10 vent. Vents are rated on a loose scale from 0-10 where 10 is the highest point of anger and frustration and 0 is a level where there's no emotion, hence, no need to vent. It's useful to check in with ourselves prior to any vent and know what level we're on. If we're at a 10 with our emotional status, it's good to let the Witness know that we're in a Dark Vent. Dark Vents generally range from 8-10 while standard vents range from 1-7. Let's look at the Venting Scale in more detail.

Venting Scale

- LEVEL 0 — I may or may not be aware of a particular situation and have zero emotion around said situation; thus, no need to vent.
- LEVEL 1 — I'm aware of the situation, but there's no real emotion associated with it; thus, there's really no need to vent unless we intellectually understand the situation should be vented about (i.e., it's bothered us in the past or is related to another situation that did trigger us).
- LEVEL 2 — I'm aware of the situation, but I'm not sure what I really feel about it. Generally, when we're not sure what emotions we're feeling or if we're not sure if we're feeling emotions, we usually are feeling something. We may be out of touch with those feelings or are somehow disconnected from that part of ourselves. Venting will often allow these feelings to come to the surface more clearly.
- LEVEL 3 — I'm aware of the situation and am definitely triggered and I feel some emotion around it, but I can be alright with the emotions I'm feeling and don't have a strong need to address those emotions right now.
- LEVEL 4 — The situation is bothering me and I'd like to address this feeling now.
- LEVEL 5 — This situation is bothering me and I'd like to focus on the source of the trigger and emotions. I'm also in a

space of actually blaming others for how I'm feeling and am assigning myself the victim role.

- LEVEL 6 — I'm extremely agitated and feel that others should feel what I'm feeling as a form of justice and a way for me to feel better.

- LEVEL 7 — I'm deep in emotion and pain to the point where I don't know all the emotions I'm feeling right now. I feel like the victim for sure, but I would like to be the villain and inflict pain on the person(s) triggering me as a sense of justice and way to feel better and more empowered. I feel hurting the person(s) who triggered me is justified.

- LEVEL 8 — I'm pissed or deeply depressed and not really in a rational or analytical mental space right now. Others need to help me before I go off on everyone, whether they're involved in the situation or not. I don't care about what I am or my ability to move out of how I feel, as I'd rather witness others hurting as a form of justice.

- LEVEL 9 — I don't want to hear anyone or anything right now. I don't know what I'll do, but whatever it is, it won't be pretty whether to myself or others.

- LEVEL 10 — F*ck everything and everyone. I'm dead serious. Life isn't fair, so I'm not going to be either. No consideration for anyone or anything right now. Try me if you want too. Consequences means absolutely nothing to me right now and I have no fear. I'm a danger to myself and others.

This rating scale also becomes important when we consider that after venting, we can check in and notice that our emotional level has gone down. The level of rage and anger, sadness, and even unhappiness can be diminished when we're allowed to express those emotions. Ratings also come in handy when we need to find out just how much emotion we're feeling, give it a number, and embrace what IS.

"Communication involves self-revelation on the part of one individual and listening on the part of another."

— Dr. Gary Chapman

Who Is the Witness?

Let's take a moment to talk about choosing the Witness of a vent as referenced in Steps 3 and 4. Remember, these are human beings with feelings, emotions, opinions, traumas, and potential triggers just like us. Ideally, a Witness will center within their Higher Self consciousness when holding space for a venting person because it allows the Witness to be there in love and support, rather than in Ego. Deliberately choosing to remain in Higher Self allows the Witness to see the bigger picture of what the vent is without taking things personally. We can only do that when we're in the Higher Self consciousness. The Animal and Ego aren't capable of showing up in full support because they're focused on themselves. However, it is a challenge to show up in Higher Self; thus, it takes practice. It helps when we've vented multiple times ourselves because it gives us the perspective on why it's best to remain neutral and show up in love.

The Witness is there for the person venting. They're there for support, love, and understanding in a world where the Animal is rarely understood or accepted. For this reason, the Witness is playing a crucial role in facilitating healing for the person venting. It takes energy, focus, and desire to be a Witness, so it's not something that should be taken lightly. In Step 7, the Witness takes on the responsibility for soothing the person venting by either offering empathy, touch, reassurance, or a simulation. The

Witness should offer this to the person venting as a show of support and a willingness and desire to be there. Let's look at each of these soothing methods.

How to Soothe the Animal and Appease the Ego as a Witness

Empathy means a Witness is showing full understanding of what a venting person is feeling by offering examples of similar experiences that are directly related to what the person venting has gone through. To show empathy properly, a Witness must (a) declare an understanding of how the person venting feels and (b) offer examples and proof they can relate to what's been shared. Too often, we say we understand when we really don't, and that, in itself, can be triggering. The job of the Witness is to offer support in a time of need. The burden isn't on the person venting because they know what they're saying is a lie and coming from their Animal (container was set). A venting person doesn't have to apologize for being vulnerable or raw after setting container because the venting person is the one in need. The work here is for the Witness to facilitate healing and hold space. The Witness's job is to convince the person venting that they understand and empathize with the situation. This is why we must ask someone to be a Witness before we vent because they have to be in the right headspace to do it. It's a responsibility.

Keep in mind that empathy isn't advice or an attempting to make the venting person cheer up, feel better, or get over it. Empathy means understanding by putting oneself into the shoes of the venting person. Empathy means getting into the feeling along with the venting person, feeling what they might be feeling, letting a venting person know that we deeply understand what they're feeling while reserving judgment or classification of any kind. Here's an example: Someone might vent about feeling loveless, alone, and afraid. The

Witness giving empathy will express how terrible that must feel and how loneliness is incredibly hard to manage. A seasoned Witness may even recount a story from their life about how it felt to be in a similar position, how depression sneaks up and takes over, and how awful it must be to feel depressed and alone.

Another important note about Empathy is that we shouldn't utilize the space to apologize or to defend ourselves. Empathy isn't about defense or explaining ourselves, as if the vent were about us, the Witness. Apologies aren't necessary in the UPLVL Communication™ System at all, unless one is asked to Simulate an apology. (We discuss the meaning of a simulation below). Why are apologies not seen as an effective way to give empathy?

A. Because when we apologize, we're doing so from a sense of having done something wrong. The Progressive Love™ Tenets state that there is to be no shame or blame, and there are no victims or villains, so no one is wrong.

B. The ventor has already set container, wherein it is noted that this is the Ego speaking on behalf of the Animal, thus, no one is wrong. It's just a vent, after all and essentially a lie.

Empathy means to place yourself into the shoes of another as opposed to defending or discussing oneself at all. In fact, it's best to stay focused on the person venting rather than injecting yourself into the supposed empathy, unless you're giving examples of how you can relate to their triggers.

Touch means to be physically soothing to the person venting. Depending on the Witness's relationship to the venting person, touch can be a hug, long embrace, or head rub. It's really up to the person venting to let the Witness know where and how they'd like to be touched and it's especially loving to ask the Venting person if they would like touch and how they want to be touched. This is important because the person venting knows where it hurts and how they'd like to be soothed. Touching them the wrong way or in the wrong area can be counterproductive. If the person venting doesn't suggest where they'd like to be touched and how, it's up to the Witness to ask. If they're not sure, a hug is suggested.

Reassurance means letting someone know it's going to be alright. That no matter how bad things may be, there will be better days ahead and we're going to get through this together. Sometimes, we just need someone else to help us see the sunlight when we're seemingly trapped in the darkness.

A **Simulation** is when we act out a scenario that soothes the person who's venting. For example, if someone vents about their Animal feeling hurt because they're not receiving enough compliments from their partner, they can ask for a simulation in which their partner gives them a compliment on their clothing or hair. Even though this is done within the context of a simulation, it still feels good to the Animal. This is because the Animal part of us doesn't really know the difference between a simulation and a real-life scenario because it all feels the same. If someone tells us they love us, it feels good regardless of the context in which it was said. That's just how the human brain is built. The statement itself will have a soothing effect regardless of context. Again, a Witness has to be within their Higher Self in order to do these simulations because they will often go against what they would normally do. In the example above, the Witness may not be the kind of person who offers compliments; therefore, coming out of their shell to offer it to the person venting may be triggering and a challenge. A side note is that the challenge of simulating an action, words, or deeds will always develop the Witness by creating a powerful opening for personal growth and development.

Open-ended questions can also be used as a soothing method after a vent. Often, when we vent, we want to know the Witness has an interest in what we're saying, and one indication of this is when a Witness has questions about what's being vented about. For example, we may vent about not feeling appreciated in our relationship. The Witness can request to ask an open-ended question to gain more clarity on what's been said thus far. After the vent, the Witness might say, "Can I ask you an open-ended question?" If the person venting says yes, the Witness can proceed to ask a focused question. For example, "You said you didn't feel appreciated for all the work you do for our relationship, but why do you feel compliments and shows of love don't count as appreciation?" Or maybe the question could be, "When was the first time you felt like I didn't appreciate you?"

Asking these types of open-ended questions can help the person get out more of their thoughts by really feeling heard by the Witness. These questions also help the Witness gain a perspective on how the Animal of the ventor is feeling.

Open-ended questions can also be used by the venting person to soothe the Animal. For instance, if a husband allows a wife to set container and vent, the wife might ask open-ended questions like "Why does it seem so difficult for you to give me compliments?" or "Do you think I'm beautiful?"

Note: The only suitable response to answers given to an open-ended question is "Thank you for answering" or "Thank you for sharing." This technique is part of the UPLVL Communication™ system because it reduces arguments by leaving the questions "open";

meaning, in many cases not answered to the satisfaction of the Ego. Generally we're afraid to answer questions when in the heat of a vent due to the propensity to go back and forth, in circles, about what was said, how it was said, and whether or not we like the response. Deciding that we will respond with a standard reply like "Thank you for sharing" ensures safety and is part of the container that keeps arguments to a minimum. This response also allows us to take a breath in between shares and truly hear the other person instead of thinking of our next response.

A Witness can go back and forth providing empathy, touch, reassurance, and simulations in response to (and initiation of) open-ended questions until the ventor feels heard and is down to a low level of emotion or not feeling triggered at all.

> "To effectively communicate, we must realize that we are all different in the way we perceive the world and use this understanding as a guide to our communication with others."
>
> —Tony Robbins

Setting Container

In Step 5, we set container. The first key to venting effectively is to set container. A container is a language tool that lets everyone who will hear the vent know that the vent is coming from the Animal via the Ego, and, as such, isn't a true depiction of our character, higher mind, or rational voice. A vent is just an animalistic expression and most importantly, the expression isn't rooted in rational reality; it's rather a LIE or false, Ego-based, narrative from the Animal, who isn't a rational thinker.

So, when we set container, we answer the question *who is speaking*.

Take a moment to imagine your worst enemy in front of you. Someone whom you perceive to have robbed you of your value, stolen something important to you, and ruined your life! Now imagine being able to sit before them and allow your Animal expression to come forth, fully raw and unfiltered. Imagine being able to scream at them, fight them, and tear them apart limb by limb. Now imagine that you have done this and the feeling of total release is upon you. You feel venerated, heard, seen, witnessed in your anger, and yet, the person you have vented to is untouched. Yes! All of your malice and pain was unleashed right before them, it felt like you were tearing them apart limb by limb, and there they are, sitting still, and hearing you, even telling you that they understand, you're fully heard, and your feelings are noted and important.

Most cannot imagine being heard and acknowledged in such a safe space, but the venting practice is such a thing and it's the setting of container that makes this possible. Setting container has many forms, and one can do this based on personal language choices, but it's a series of words that allows the Witness who will hear the vent to know that this expression isn't personal. The series of words that make up a container will not only create a safe space for everyone involved but also allow the Animal to be in full expression without holding back, which is the entire point of venting to begin with.

So, how do we create container? We do the following:

1. Ask if we can vent.
2. If the person says "Yes" then we set container by acknowledging who is speaking. For example, "Thanks for allowing me to vent. I'm acknowledging that this is my Animal speaking through my Ego and that no one is doing anything wrong to

me. You're not wrong and I'm not blaming you at all. I simply feel like my Animal needs to be heard."

That's it. The container has officially been set and now it's safe to vent. Note that both these steps are important. It's the asking of permission to vent that sends the initial signal that we are simply going through an exercise and that no one is being castigated. Asking permission to vent also gives the Witness power and choice and makes the overall venting practice a mutually beneficial exercise with two empowered individuals participating. When we need to vent, we cannot force anyone to hear it. Asking for permission lets us know that we have a willing Witness. If a potential Witness says no, it's time to find another Witness.

Venting Nuts and Bolts

Step 6 is the actual Vent. When we allow Ego to share the actual emotions of the Animal in any given scenario (work, home, or community), we actually are becoming vulnerable and open with others. Showing others what we really think and how we really feel is a vulnerable act in a culture that hasn't allowed it for centuries. When we first introduce this technology called Venting to our clients, they feel a sense of fear, shame, and even self-loathing when asked to actually allow the Animal to speak, allow their Ego to give that Animal a voice! But rapidly, they realize the empowering place we open when we share vulnerably with others and express raw emotion. What our clients pull upon are the memories of keeping their Animal emotions contained to a diary. Journaling is one way our culture has responded to the need to vent. But once the diary was found by a parent, the trouble that ensued made us wonder if it's safe anywhere to vent. We've specifically learned to bottle up emotion because our own powerful and raw selves aren't welcomed anywhere on the planet!

Another concern around venting, which is a real concern, is that violence, hatred, or even exile await on the other side of such expressions. When our parents found the journal or when we took a risk and belted out our feelings in what was considered an inappropriate manner, we were punished. This instilled in us a massive fear of connection to others, which stands at the core of the basic human needs spectrum. Solitary confinement is a form of torture because it's critical for humans to connect with one another. So, if sharing Animal emotions will cause us to be removed from society and punished with aloneness, then, by all means, we'll suppress them. Moreover, if physical violence accompany the emotional violence of separation from the group, then this behavior of Ego sharing Animal's emotive expression must assuredly be stopped. Our clients have to move past this fear, as it simply doesn't have to be the case. This fear is quelled when we demonstrate the total UPLVL Communication™ system with our clients. Our clients discover the power of taking a good vent and releasing it from the body in the company of peers. So, what is a good vent?

A good vent includes emotion. We don't try to speak softly, suppress anger, or hide sadness. Crying is allowed, screaming is allowed, having a table-pounding tantrum is welcomed in fact! A good vent truly releases the energy of the emotion from the body. Its organic and raw; it's not at all necessary to be good, nice, agreeable, or mannerly. Cursing is great in a vent, even for youth, speaking in whatever language the Ego sees fit when sharing the Animal's feelings and thoughts is perfect. In corporate environments, there must be space set aside for this form of communication, as it isn't usually part of corporate culture. If space is created in corporate settings for venting, there would be a change in the culture for the better. Families and homes would become highly connective places where venting is allowed, but the vent must be visceral, real, powerful, and freely allowed. This is the key: freely allowed. How do we allow such a thing in these kinds of environments that have historically been closed to such activity? We set container.

"Much unhappiness has come into the world because of bewilderment and things left unsaid."

— Fyodor Dostoevsky

Open-Ended Questions

We mentioned open-ended questions being a great tool for soothing someone who has just vented, but they're also a great tool for allowing the Animal to express itself by appealing to its curious nature. An old saying insists that curiosity killed the cat, but that's only outside of a safe space and container. The cat can be as curious as it wants to be inside of a proper UPLVL Communication™ container and when it's with supportive people. The point is, animals have a curious nature about them, and that nature exists within us as well. The way we feed our curiosity is through open-ended questions. They are called open-ended because once they are answered, the conversation is then closed. There is no circular back and forth with an open-ended question, which means, most likely, the question won't get answered to our satisfaction, which is why they're considered "open." There's usually so much more the Ego wants to know; thus, it engages in requests for clarification, refuting the answers given, or acting emotionally to the answers given until either an argument ensues or it simply draws a line in the sand and refuses to discuss things further (i.e., closed). "Closed" means the discussion ends with a circular back and forth until either: (a) the Ego is satisfied, (b) the Animal is satisfied, (c) the Animal shuts down, (d) the Ego refuses to listen and be open to any more input from the other person, (e) a blow up occurs and irreparable damage takes place, (f) a physical confrontation happens, or (g) things are elevated to a traumatic level at which the hurt and pain from the argument or discussion becomes something we must recover and heal ourselves from. This is a "closed ended" discussion because it's going to come to an end (i.e., be closed out), but the question is how exactly will that happen if we don't acknowledge the Ego is speaking and the Animal is reacting? Yes, ideally, we close the discussion with scenarios (a) and (b), but the point of this book is that that's not usually the case, especially during the most critical times in a relationship. By leaving the questions and discussion "open," we allow the best chance for the Ego to at least be partially satisfied, if not totally, and we give the Animal enough soothing and attention for it to feel safe, thus, allowing us to bring reason and rationality back into the relationship. Remember that the vent is a lie and, therefore, any questions around that vent won't provide anything of any real substance, but it will help satisfy our curiosity, which is very soothing to the Animal within us.

How it works is the person venting may still feel triggered after their vent is complete and even after they've received soothing from the Witness in the form of empathy, touch, reassurance, or simulation. In that case, the venting party can set container again and ask the Witness if they can ask an open-ended question. The Witness can again choose to either agree to hear the question and answer it or to not receive the question. Here's how the conversation may go.

> Person Venting: "Jason, may I ask you an open-ended question? You haven't done anything wrong. This is just to soothe my Animal's curiosity."

Witness (Jason): "Yes, you may."

Person Venting: "Why did you call Marsha when I was asleep the other night?"

Witness (Jason): "I felt like it."

Person Venting: "Thank you for sharing."

This is the end for that particular question. The first thing to notice is that the answer given was short and generally unsatisfactory. Without us even knowing the scenario, we can all agree there's more being sought from the Person Venting than the answer that Jason gave, but that's just tough. Jason answered in a way he felt was true and authentic and whether the Person Venting agrees or not, they'll have to be satisfied. However, they're free to ask another question if the Witness is up for it, but they have to inquire if the can ask again. Additionally, they can't ask the same question over again. Maybe the next open-ended question goes like this:

Person Venting: "May I ask you another open-ended question? This is purely for the satisfaction of my Animal and Ego. You haven't done anything wrong.

Witness (Jason): "Yes, you may."

Person Venting: "Do my feelings matter to you?"

Witness (Jason): "Yes, your feelings do matter to me. I really care about how you feel and I personally don't like it when you're hurting or in pain in any way. I also sometimes wish I knew how to soothe you better whenever you're triggered, or, better yet, I'd love to know how to not trigger you so often. That makes me feel bad about myself because who wants to be the source of their partner's hurt and pain. I don't know. I just wish the best for you always."

Person Venting: "Thank you for sharing."

As we can see here, the Witness went more in depth with their answer and probably gave the Person Venting more than they were looking for. Here the Witness went into their feelings and shared some of the emotions they felt whenever they triggered their partner. Sometimes, when questions are asked, the Witness flows with exactly how they feel and may go off on a tangent just a bit. The point is, we never know what we'll get when asking an open-ended question. Essentially, when asking an open-ended question, we allow the Witness to step out of observation and Higher Self and into their own Ego. Interestingly enough, the Person Venting will have to be in Higher Self as much as possible when listening to these answers. Yes, it's the Animal's curiosity that we're trying to satisfy, but the answers are potential triggers. If we're going to check and see what's downstairs in the dark basement, we're going to have to better ready ourselves for whatever avails itself. However, overall, it's better to have answers to our Ego-based questions than not and it essentially soothes the Ego to be able to ask freely the questions of the Animal. After all, a moaning cat who could use words might ask for milk (simulation) and after drinking the milk might ask why her human was so late providing the milk. Now, the moaning stops, and the cat, feeling heard and seen, begins to feel soothed.

Counter Venting

Venting doesn't have to be a one-side affair when only one person is venting and only one person is being the Witness. People can vent to each other in a ping-pong fashion. This is called Counter Venting. All of the same rules apply from the single venting exercise and there's no interrupting each other during the vents. This prevents an Egoic argumentative type of interaction from taking place. This is a great way for a couple to express their Animal emotions and triggers in a safe space and without anyone feeling the need to get defensive.

Via a counter vent, a Witness, after holding space for a ventor, can then set container and do their own vent! In this way, we open space for a dance of sorts, wherein both parties can allow the Animal some space to just be seen and heard. It's important to utilize each step, not skip components of the UPLVL Communication™ venting exercise, and remain ordered in the sharing. This might seem robotic, at first, to include so many transitional statements, questions, and container setting, but this is the end of the modern argument, which has always been a fruitless kind of communication with no clear set boundaries, objectives, or inborn kindnesses.

Warning About Soothing the Ego

In our modern, Western culture, we're not used to feeling soothed when we're in our Animal, allowing Ego to vent out. Often, it takes practice to begin feeling soothed by Empathy, Touch, Simulation and/or Reassurance. Even Open-Ended Questions can lead to battles when we don't properly respond to an answer given, or when a response to such a question triggers us all over again. It's important to note that it takes time to begin to learn what it actually feels like to be heard, seen, soothed, and such. This is a journey that begins the first time we set container and vent. We are learning to trust the Witness and to trust ourselves. Feeling soothed is a journey. Often, we believe we cannot be soothed. Often, we don't want to feel soothed because the feeling is so foreign to us. Keep this in mind as you begin this journey into deeper more powerful communication. UPLVL Communication™ is a mindfulness practice that eventually shows us who we are and the potential we have as humans. Begin your practice by realizing where you are and what you still must discover about communication.

Venting Case Studies

Let's look at some venting examples so we can see how it works.

Case Study #1: In this example, a husband is mad that his wife didn't tell him that she used to date one of his friends from college. He found out through another mutual friend at a party just last night and they've been married for twelve years.

> Husband: "I'd like to vent right now. Are you willing to hold space for me at this time?"
>
> Wife: "Yes, I'm willing to hold space for you right now."
>
> Husband: "Thank you. You've done nothing wrong. This is my Ego speaking on behalf of my inner Animal. I realize everything I'm about to say is a lie and without any rational basis. It's just I feel my Animal needs to be heard right now.

What the entire F*CK!!! You used to date one of my homeboys and never felt the need to tell me? I just feel like that's some f*cked up sh*t, like for real, for real. I'm so pissed right now and embarrassed. I don't know who I feel betrayed by more — you or him. Why wouldn't either of you think I might want know that information?! Dude is at my wedding giving out toasts and sh*t and you all have this secret and I'm none the wiser. I feel like a fool to know that you two are sitting up there with your history together and what's even more disturbing is that I know other people know about it and were probably too embarrassed to tell me. I feel like an idiot. Where's the trust? Where's the truthfulness? And on top of all that, I don't know what else is even a lie in our relationship right now? Is there anything else? I guess it doesn't make sense to ask because I'm sure you wouldn't tell me anyway. I just don't know what to do right now. I'm at a total loss for words or actions. I feel like taking a trip somewhere and just forgetting about everything for a month. This really sucks. I guess I'm just hurt by this. There's really nothing I can do about it now, but I do feel like kicking his ass to keep it real though. I still might, but I guess we'll see. I guess that's all I had to say."

Wife: "You are heard. What can I do to support you right now?"

Husband: "I really don't know. Maybe you can do a simulation where you come to me after we decide to be together and you tell me about you and him having been in a relationship."

Wife: "Okay. Listen, I'm so happy that we've decided to be together and I'm really hoping that we'll be together forever, but I want to put everything on the table now before we get too far down the road in this relationship. The first thing is that your friend and I were in a brief relationship together about a year ago. It's something that just happened. We met each other at a party and hit it off. We ended up dating for about two months, but it was clear it wasn't a match so we broke it off. Yes, we did have sex. I just wanted you to know that."

Husband: "Thank you for that simulation. It feels good to hear you tell me the truth at the time when I would have wanted to hear it. It's still painful to hear it, but I appreciate it. Thank you."

Wife: "You're welcome. Is there any other way I can support you."

Husband: "Yes, I could really use a hug right now."

Wife: Proceeds to hug and hold husband.

End of Venting Exercise

There are a few observations we should take away from this example. First, the husband was both angry and deeply hurt by the scenario he vented about. During his vent, his Animal directed the anger at the wife and best friend. This is what the Animal does. It must attack someone when it's in a state of discomfort because it doesn't have the capability of rationalizing how exactly it got the point of feeling the way it does. The Ego is similar in that it looks to blame someone else for its perceived failures. The Ego never sees itself as the source of its perceived shortcomings. It can't bear to be witnessed in a bad light. The Progressive Love™ tenets the husband stands outside of are: No Victims, No Villains, No Blame, The Purpose is Growth, The Benefit is Love, and I Create My Life so the vent is definitely justified and needed. Venting starts the process of moving back to center and balance and thus our power.

The next observation is that even though the wife was the subject of the vent, she stood in love and acceptance of her husband. She could have easily gotten into her Ego or Animal about the words he was saying to her, but she understood who was talking thanks to him setting container. This is the proper way to be a Witness for someone venting. When we're unable to do this, it's best to not hear the vent until we can be in our Higher Self.

It should also be noted that the husband was able to withhold his criticisms until after he set container. This is how we avoid circular arguments and conflict inside of relationships. This is how we avoid resentment and actually preserve the relationship for the long term.

The husband wasn't immediately soothed after his wife did the simulation and asked for additional support in the form of a hug. But the key here is the wife asked him if he needed additional support beyond the simulation, which is exactly what a Witness should be doing in this instance. The key is being there to help the person who's venting feel better and get out all the Animal and Ego communication and feelings during the vent session. This is great work on her part and great work on his part to be open to asking for what he felt he needed. His vulnerability is the key to making this venting practice effective.

Case Study #2: In this example, a wife suspects that her husband has cheated on her. The wife's friend sent her a picture of the husband out with another woman and being intimate with her (i.e., holding hands and kissing).

Wife: "I have to f*cking vent right now! I need you to hear me out. Are you willing to do that?"

Husband: "Yes I am."

Wife: "You've done nothing wrong. This is just my Ego and Animal speaking. I know I create my life and that no one is doing anything to me. It's just my Ego and Animal need to be heard right now.

What the ENTIRE f*ck do you think you're doing f*cking with another woman and we're married?!?! I can't believe you're doing this to me and our family. You've never cared about anything or anyone other than yourself. You've always been a selfish bastard. I knew I shouldn't have married you. My mother even told me not to marry you because you looked like a sneaky son of a b*tch. F*ck You!!! Who is this b*tch you were with? Was she the only one? How long have you been seeing her? You better start talking right the f*ck now. I'm outta here and I'm not coming back. You can have the car and the house and wait for my lawyer to contact you. You really f*cked up this time. Who would have thought you were like these other jack*sses out here running the streets with any old h*e you can find. Now, all my friends are talking about me and us and we look like a couple of jack*sses right now. I hate you! I hate you!! I f*cking HATE you!!! I'm outta here."

The wife storms out of the room, crying. She slams the door and throws a vase against the wall, breaking it then jumps on the bed, curled up and crying.

Husband: "Baby, please let me hold you. Sweetie, I completely understand you're pissed right now and I know this is some bullsh*t that I'm putting you through right now. I get that and I understand how bad this must hurt. I've definitely felt betrayed like this in the past and I was pissed and hurt all at the same time."

The husband lays next to his wife and holds her. She's resistant at first, but then allows him to console her.

Ending of the Vent Exercise

There are a number of observations to make with Case Study #2. First of all, the wife was barely able to set container because of how angry her Animal and Ego were, but she managed to do it, which is a major accomplishment for a trigger as serious as being cheated on. But in setting container, it allowed the husband to show up for her in the best way possible without himself being triggered and defensive. Next, the formal venting exercise broke down at the end of the wife's vent. She left the room, broke stuff, slammed the door, and retreated to her bed. She was in no state of mind to ask for soothing. She wasn't really in a state of mind to receive support as she was still in a deep emotional state.

After the wife vented, the husband offered touch and empathy even though the wife didn't specifically ask for it. This is great because his effort is what's important. He realized she was outside of the formal venting exercise and did his best to continue following the process. Although she was initially resistant to the soothing he had to offer, he was eventually able to support her. This is ad-libbing as best he can.

NOTE: Often, we'll experience behavior from someone's Animal or Ego outside of any formal venting exercise, but that's not an excuse to attempt to discard the UPLVL Communication™ process. The truth is, most experiences with our Animal will be outside of any structure, and that's okay. If we can stay aware and inside of our Higher Self, we can help to de-escalate situations by applying the tools when we can. Or sometimes we start out within the UPLVL Communication™ structure, but somehow fall into chaos. That's okay too. Just do your best to apply tools whenever you can.

It should be noted that the wife's vent can be categorized as a Dark Vent, which means she technically should have warned her husband in advance. That said, warnings won't always happen when emotions run high. It was definitely a Level 10. Not only were her words aggressive and accusatory, but her behavior was harsh as well. This is okay too because the Animal wants to express itself in this kind of animated way. The Animal isn't just verbal, but physical as well, throwing a vase against a wall is perfectly within reason and to be expected. The same applies to slamming doors or jumping into the bed and crying uncontrollably. We have to realize that we're dealing with genuine Animal nature here, and there's some real pain that needs to be expressed and released from the body. In other words, although the UPLVL Communication™ protocols are structured and formal, the Animal has no desire to stick to that structure. Yes, the Ego can stay within the structure, but it won't always be able to express the Animal in a formal, structured way, and that's okay.

Case Study #3: In this example, someone has been passed up for promotion for the third time by someone they feel isn't as skilled or deserving as them. In this specific example, we're going to assume the employees at the company are trained in the UPLVL Communication™ protocols; thus, the employee is going to vent to their supervisor. This vent can take place during a special meeting between the supervisor and employee or during a formal evaluation.

Employee: "I'd like to vent about the recent decision to pass me over for promotion. Are you willing to hear my vent at this time?"

Supervisor: "Yes, I'm willing to hear your vent."

Employee: "You haven't done anything wrong. This is strictly my Ego speaking. My Ego feels like it needs to be heard, but I fully understand that I create my life and no one is doing anything to me.

I'm hurt and disappointed that I got passed over for promotion yet again. I have the longest tenure here at the company compared to all my peers, and I feel I know the most about what it takes to be successful at the next level. My evaluation and job performance scores have been above average consistently for years. I just don't get it. I feel that other employees basically brown nose and kiss ass in order to move ahead in this company, but for those who simply follow the rules and work hard, it's never enough. This is the third time I've been passed over and it just doesn't seem fair. I have no idea what I need to do to get promoted to the next level. I'm truly at a loss right now. To be honest, I don't even feel like being here because I don't feel wanted and valued and, on top of that, I don't feel I'll even be missed if I do move on. That's it, I guess."

Supervisor: "Thanks for sharing how you feel. How can I support you?"

Employee: "I'd really like some reassurance that my efforts aren't taken for granted and that I do have the opportunity to grow my career here."

Supervisor: "You should know that myself and the rest of executive team here at the company see your work and effort as valuable. We're all confident that if you continue on your same course that you'll see advancement to the next level and beyond. We all believe in you here."

Employee: "Thank you. Could you also offer me some empathy? I feel like my Ego needs it."

Supervisor: "Of course. I for one know how it feels to want to succeed badly in my job, put the work in every day, but not feel appreciated by my boss. I've had that experience before at my previous company and grew frustrated that I didn't receive the pay raises and bonuses I felt I deserved. On top of that, I saw some of my peers, who in my opinion were underperformers, get raises and bonuses. It was hurtful to me at the time and actually still feels hurtful even to this day. So, I empathize with how you're feeling right now."

Employee: "Thank you. That feels better."

Supervisor: "You're welcome."

End of Venting Exercise

There are a few observations we can make in this case study. First, the Supervisor never apologies for not promoting the Employee because they're not actually being blamed for anything and there's absolutely no reason for feeling guilty or bad about anything. This is a venting exercise and the Employee's Ego is speaking from their personal hurt, pain, and perspective. The Employee's vent is by no means an indictment on the Supervisor.

The Supervisor does a great job of not getting defensive or in their feelings during the Employee's vent.

The Employee did a great job of ending the vent by saying, "That's it." It's important to clearly end a vent so that the Witness doesn't prematurely interrupt before the vent is complete. It's not always easy to end a vent because we may still be in our feelings, but when we can, it helps the exercise to go much smoother. Furthermore, there's no need to end a vent prior to feeling a sense of completeness. If there's a long pause during a vent, the Witness is welcome to ask if they're finished venting. Never assume a vent it done.

The Employee also did a great job of asking for additional support in the form of empathy. The point of the Witness offering this support is to soothe the venter so offering multiple soothing methods is to be expected.

Lastly, the Employee asks for reassurance from the Supervisor that their efforts were appreciated. We need to reiterate that the vent is a *figurative lie* and both the person venting and Witness know this. From that standpoint, we shouldn't feel conflicted about offering reassurance that isn't *truthful* either. Meaning, when the Supervisor reassured the Employee that their efforts were appreciated and that they were on a path for promotion, that may or may not have been actually true, and that's okay. The point is that the Employee needed to feel reassured in that moment and that's what they received. That's the most important thing — to soothe the Animal and Ego so that the Higher Self can settle in and proceed with creating the life they desire. If the Employee wants a formal performance evaluation or to talk about their future, they can set up a meeting with the Supervisor outside of the Venting and UPLVL Communication™ exercise. The point here is to appease the Animal so performance isn't adversely affected and ensure a nontoxic work environment.

There shouldn't be any conflict with this. This is actually true for all of the soothing methods in that they may or may not be "true." We know the Simulations aren't true because they're simply made-up scenarios that the Ego needs to hear. We know that Empathy may or may not be true depending on whether the Witness can truly relate to what's being vented about or even if they're in the best frame of mind to offer empathy. We know that when Touch is offered, it may not be what the Witness really wants to give at that time, but they're offering it as method to soothe the venter's Ego. We'll talk more about truth and lies in Gateway #2.

Case Study #4: In this example a relationship coach is feeling that her friend is forcing free coaching sessions on her by coming to the house and discussing her relationship life. This friend has purchased coaching from her before in the past, but has lately been trying to get free coaching by leveraging her access via their friendship.

> Coach: "Are you willing to hear me vent about a situation involving our friendship?"
>
> Friend: "Sure."
>
> Coach: "Thank you. You've done nothing wrong. This is just my Ego speaking. I just feel I need to be heard right now, but I'm totally clear that I create my life and all things serve to further my growth.
>
> I feel like you abuse our friendship and your access to me in order to get professional coaching services from me without paying. Like, you'll come over and want to talk or share something, but it's really just you talking about one of your relationship problems and asking me for my opinion on

it. That's basically what I do for a living. I listen to people talk about their relationships then I offer compassion, comfort, and solutions to help them move forward in the best way possible. What irritates me the most is that I feel you know this because you've paid for coaching services from me before where we've had the exact same conversations that you're trying to have for free on the sly. That's how I feel about it. I just don't think friends treat each other that way. I don't want to cut off our friendship, but I feel that's the only way to really set the proper boundaries. That's all."

Friend: "Thank you for sharing. How can I support you?"

Coach: "I'd appreciate some empathy from you right now."

Friend: "I totally understand where you're coming from when you say you feel I'm abusing my status as a friend to get free coaching. I feel like I've had the same experience with my family. Like, my cousin will come over to the house with her children then say she's got to run a quick errand but not come back until nighttime. It feels abusive every time she does it and I feel like she knows better. It's annoying. My children are grown and out of the house. Whenever I needed to do something when I had small children, I would get a babysitter or ask explicitly if family or friends could watch them. I also tried to be sensitive to their time and space and not overdue how much I leveraged them. So, yeah. I think I know how you feel in this situation."

Coach: "Thank you. That felt good."

Friend: "Do you need further support?"

Coach: "No. I feel heard."

End of the Venting Exercise

The primary observations from Case Study #4 were that the Friend refrained from apologizing. There's never a need to apologize because the vent is a lie and coming from the Ego so it's simply not a universal truth that will apply across the board. Secondly, the Friend here offered a really great example of how she had gone through a similar thing where she felt like her status with family was used to abuse her. It's critically important to use situations that are close to what's being vented about so that the person venting knows that they're understood.

But How Do We Decide Who Is Right or Wrong

Now that we've viewed four case studies, we might be asking ourselves who the winner of the argument is? Who is the winner and who is the loser? How do we find out who to punish and who is guilty of the crime?

UPLVL Communication™ is a system that discards the concept of right and wrong, good or bad; it dissolves the duality we perpetually hold into place using old language technology. The venting party is never wanting to guilt or shame the Witness, even when the Witness is the person who triggered the venter. We must realize that becoming triggered isn't a problem. No argument needs to ensue and we don't have to shame or blame anyone due to feeling triggered or uncomfortable.

Yes, we promote venting, getting the feelings and thoughts of the Animal out of the body. In fact, when done well, this process promotes vulnerability and, actually, intimacy with the Witness. A venting person is allowing their self to be seen and heard, witnessed in their vulnerable moment of anger, pain, depression, sadness, or extreme joy or anxiety! The aim is never to make anyone feel wrong or bad, but rather to open up, share, express oneself and become accustomed to allowing the Animal a voice.

As you embark upon your UPLVL Communication™ journey, remain keenly aware that we're shifting ourselves and how we think, not just how we speak. We're thinking in new ways when we set container and vent. We're saying that no one is wrong. So, we essentially end any foreseeable disagreement before it begins. This should feel soothing to us. This should help us feel safe and held in the arms of others rather than angry and frustrated. We can state our case, realize it's not actually true, but be heard either way and ask for the support we need to calm down instead of being told curtly to calm down before we've had a chance to share our deepest, most primal selves with one another. This is a viable way to get to know one another more deeply and show one another we care.

"The single biggest problem in communication is the illusion that it has taken place."

— George Bernard Shaw

Gateway #2 — PROCESSING

Processing is the next step to take after venting. It's critically important to vent because venting makes processing possible. When we vent, we release the surface concerns and calm the Animal down. Now our Higher Self can actually consider the truth of the matter — I Create My Life. When we explode and rage, cry and scream and allow the Animal its due, we find a place of calm in the soothing that follows. We find a place to finally ask the question: How Did I Create This?

Processing is the exercise of identifying where our emotional triggers are sourced. Processing asks the question, "Which part of myself, my past, my trauma is the pain point and source of why I was emotionally triggered?" We know that we are the source because via the Progressive Love™ Tenet — I create my life — we are the source of everything that takes place in our lives. Our pleasures come from within. Our happiness comes from within. Our resolve, confidence, compassion, self-esteem, self-worth, and love for the world all comes from within; so does our pain, triggers, and pain points. How do we know this? Because we can do the same thing to Person A and Person B and they have completely different reactions and responses; therefore, we've proven that the outside event isn't the source of our responses (i.e., feelings and emotions), but, rather, our internal stories and relationship to the events. Processing, therefore, is the practice of identifying (a) what our story is around the event that triggered us and (b) where that story relative to the triggering event was birthed. That's essentially our work in Gateway #2.

Before we go through the Processing Gateway, we need to continue to redefine terms that we've assimilated over the course of our lifetime. We need to make sure we're viewing our lives from the vantage point of our Higher Self whenever possible and not allowing our Ego to mislabel reality for its own selfish purposes. This is critical because we're talking about communication with others in a way that leads to peace, harmony, and understanding as opposed to circular arguments. We must get out of the ideology of winning arguments and debates with loved ones as a method to maintain a relationship. The goal of each experience, whether painful or pleasurable, is growth, compassion, and building stronger bonds. The goal is love per our Progressive Love™ Tenets.

We need a bit more clarity on the Higher Self before we move into the depths of the Processing Gateway because Processing is all about the Higher Self. It can be said that Processing is one of the languages of the Higher Self via the Ego. There's an unseen intelligence that governs life that tends to run in the background without very much acknowledgment. It's profound in so many ways, but it's also sometimes hard to grasp. For example, inside our bodies are organs and systems that run with amazing intelligence and precision and with absolutely no input from our thinking minds. The heart, lungs, liver, kidneys, spleen, nervous system, lymph nodes, and hypothalamus all run seamlessly together in a way that computer programmers could only dream of achieving, but what is the intelligence behind their flawless operation? What are the laws governing this unseen reality?

There are nine basic laws that govern all of creation. Those laws are:

- Law 1: The Law of Power & Conservation
- Law 2: The Law of Duality & Commerce
- Law 3: The Law of Creativity & Abundance
- Law 4: The Law of Presence & Choice
- Law 5: The Law of Peace & Detachment
- Law 6: The Law of Commitment & Will
- Law 7: The Law of Wisdom & Purpose
- Law 8: The Law of Beauty & Acceptance
- Law 9: The Law of Perseverance & Justice

We could begin to consider the basic laws of the Universe by observing that they are captured in the laws of physics, metaphysics, chemistry, and so on, but they are obviously beyond our human sciences. These laws not only operate our bodies, but also feed into our awareness and thinking. Meaning, we can and do tap into these same intelligences that run our internal systems, and when we do, we've seemingly tapped into harmony, balance, and genius. The moral of the story is that when our thinking is aligned with our Higher Self, things tend to work out for the best for all parties involved. We find harmony, peace, and balance. When we talk about the Higher Self, we're talking about a universal intelligence at work in all things and within us. It's there when we sleep, eat, and in everything we do. But it's only one voice and must compete with the Ego to be heard. It must also compete with the Animal's desire to flee, fight, feed, and emote, so we can see how the voice of the Higher Self can get lost sometimes. For the purposes of UPLVL Communication™, we should know that we always have access to a super intelligence and intuitiveness within us if we're able to relax, listen to it, and trust it.

Redefining Trust

The concept of trust has been greatly misconstrued, especially when applied to relationships. The standard definition of trust is the ability of others to do what they say and to tell the truth. Meaning, if a person does what they say they're going to do, and they tell the truth at all times, then we can trust them, but if they lie or don't do what they say, then they're untrustworthy. Here's the problem, though: we've already said everything coming from the Ego is basically a lie (a subjective statement). What everyone is saying is a lie, how we're interpreting what's happening around us is a lie, and who we define ourselves and others to be is a lie too. Why? Because in almost all cases, our Ego is making these assessments. For example, labeling someone trustworthy is completely subjective and based on a limited and circumstantial experience with that person. What are our criteria for trust? Are one person's criteria for trust the same as everyone else's? If we label someone trustworthy today does it mean they'll always be trustworthy? Are we willing to bet our lives on it? I don't think so because we know we're fickle and wavering when it comes to our assessments of reality. Today, our lover is the love of our life, but tomorrow, they can be a liar and cheater. Today, our friend is our best friend for life! Tomorrow, our friend is a backstabbing, shady two-timer. Think about it, we misrepresent ourselves all the time. We definitely see this wavering energetic at play in the dating world where we put on the mask and our best face in order to set the best impression, but that's not the best representation of who we are, right? That's not even who we are most of the day, week, or month, right? No, it's who we want others to see so that others will like us and give us the benefit of the doubt. We do the same on job interviews so much so that interviewers have to add the question, "What are your weaknesses?" What they're really saying is, "Give us some insight and honesty about who you really are now so we don't fire you later on when the *real* you shows up."

We're not telling lies on purpose when we put on the shiny mask for others. We're simply allowing the Ego to show our best face or what we consider to be our best attributes. What is lying? It's the act of misrepresenting ourselves as solely the Ego when, in fact, we're a combination of Ego, Animal, and Higher Self. The Ego and Animal part of us are changeable, fickle, and largely self-centered, while our Higher Selves are constant and interested in the good of the whole. We're not our Ego and persona. How can we build trust when trust is based on telling the truth, but, at the same time, we're all misrepresenting ourselves, posing as solely Ego? How can trust be based on doing what we say we're going to do when no human being is capable of doing what they say one-hundred percent of the time, and, even when we do operate within a high percentage, we're still subject to losing the trust of another?

Let's redefine Trust as *the ability to see, note, and embrace that all experiences are perfection and are meant to grow us.* For example, saying, "I trust that you'll grow me. I trust that our relationship will grow me as well," is accurate. This is a statement from our Higher Selves and serves to give us the right perspective on life and the people we interact with.

We understand this new definition and concept of trust is a bit abstract, but try to look at it rationally for a moment. Do we trust ourselves in all areas of life? Do we trust ourselves to make the right choices with our health, money, relationships, children, leadership position, or the power positions we find ourselves in? How often do we deliver on our word versus not deliver? If we respond with a no to any of these questions, based on the old definition of trust, that we keep our word and never lie, then, of course, we don't trust ourselves. Now, let's talk to the people who don't trust us and convince them that we're trustworthy. How difficult will that be, when we don't even trust ourselves? It will be very difficult because when trust is defined and judged by the Ego, it's completely subjective and constantly subject to change. It's like a four-year-old child trying to catch a squirrel — impossible. How are we going to hold others to a trust standard when we cannot measure up to the impossible standard ourselves? We need to reassess the old definition of trust to give ourselves a fighting chance in relationships.

In the new definition of Trust as noted here in the UPLVL Communication™ System, we finally find a way to trust ourselves and everyone around us. Trust is based upon the concept that everything is always working to grow us. Every experience, communication, occurrence, or scenario is perfectly designed to take us to the next level of selfhood, and create in us a way to heal, prosper, learn, and grow. Now we trust ourselves, because we know that every choice we make, everything that has ever happened in our lives, everything we once considered a mistake was perfectly timed, placed, and executed to show us something vital about ourselves and to push us toward growth. In like manner, every action others have taken for or against us, with or without us, and every action they CAN ever take will forward our growth when viewed from the objective place of Higher Self.

> *"Trust is the glue of life. It's the most essential ingredient in effective communication. It's the foundational principle that holds all relationships."*
>
> ~ Stephen R. Covey

Lies, Truth, and Reality

For the purposes of mastering communications with one another for building better relationships, we can say Truth is Objective Reality and Lies are Subjective Reality. Objective reality means we're looking at reality from the perspective of our Higher Self, while subjective reality means we're looking at reality from the perspective of our Ego (and its counterpart the Animal). Subjective reality is a lie because it's based on one's personal perception; thus, it's not universal. How can we base truth on a reality that's perceived in different ways, by different people? We can't, but when we attempt to, we create a foundational breakdown in communication.

Let's look at examples of subjective reality that's often confused and stated as objective reality.

Typical Ego Statement: "You don't respect me."

Typical Ego Thought: It's true this person is being disrespectful toward me. It's absolutely true they don't respect me.

What is this subjective reality and perception based upon? First, it's based on the person's definition of disrespect, which will vary from person to person and scenario to scenario. Perceptions are influenced and shaped by one's past experience, as those experiences shape one's definition of disrespect. These are the same factors that shape every person's definition and perception of disrespect, but these factors are different for each person. Not only that, but because we're constantly growing and experiencing life, our individual history is constantly being rewritten; thus, our perceptions and definitions are also being rewritten. Even our own personal perspectives, subjective as they are, are being shifted daily.

What makes these statements truly false is when Ego buys into them as truth rather than simply a personal perception. Another way to state this concept is that all our venting amounts to personal perceptions that are essentially lies, the language of the Ego. Why? Because the Ego's perception is based upon the concept of separation and is challenged to see the unity in all things. The Ego's goal is to be witnessed as a unique, individual entity, apart and separate from all other things; thus, commonality and lines connecting us elude it. When we view life from the standpoint of the Ego, and subjective, personal, perspective, we're viewing a false reality, not the truth of the Higher Self, which can easily be captured in this brief affirmation: Everything Serves to Further (I Ching).

If a lie is the language of the Ego, then Truth is the language of the Higher Self. Truth is essentially Objective Reality.

A typical Higher Self declaration of truth would look like the following:

- Typical Higher Self Statement: "I am experiencing some growth through this situation wherein I feel disrespected."
- Typical Higher Self Thought: "How am I creating this? Why

am I creating this? Why do I consider this situation to be disrespectful?"

This Higher Self perspective is Objective because it's based on objective principles:

- I Create My Life.
- Everything Serves to Further.
- All experiences are set up to grow me.
- This life experience is about pleasure, peace, and pain — all of which will advance me.

Let's look at some further examples of Truth.

If we take Case Study #2 from our Venting case studies, we see a wife suspects her husband is cheating on her. The wife's friend sends her a picture of her husband with another woman at a restaurant. Let's say that she also saw text messages between her husband and the other woman to further fuel her suspicions that her husband is cheating on her.

The Ego view — He's hiding something from me.

The Higher Self View — I Create My Life. I am here to grow. How can this situation expand me? My Ego is experiencing the feeling of fear and anxiety due to my Animal's relationship to the idea of my partner loving and interacting with someone else.

Truth — I am learning to navigate situations that scare me. I am learning to be vulnerable and ask for support. I am learning to trust. I am learning to move from fear and anxiety around partners loving others to empowerment, love, and peace inside of that situation.

We can see there are major differences in the language of the Higher Self versus the Ego.

Let's look at Case Study #4 from the Venting exercise where a coach is feeling intruded on by a friend for free coaching. This friend has purchased coaching services before in the past but, in this case, has come over and seemingly forced her way into a free session.

The Ego View — She's using me!

The Higher Self View — I Create My Life. I have created this to grow me. How can this situation make me more powerful? My Ego is experiencing the feeling and perception of being used by a friend by providing them, for free, a service I normally charge for.

Truth — I am learning to truly stand up for my value. I am learning to trust my intuition. I am learning to say no. I am learning to move from the feeling of being used into empowerment, love, and peace; thus, allowing me to make authentic choices in that moment.

We can now see a very clear distinction between truth and lies and objective reality versus subjective reality. These distinctions will greatly clarify our communications by eliminating the confusion between these elements. When we review our past conversations, arguments, and discussions, we can see that they may not have gone anywhere because each person was pushing forward a lie and subjective reality as a Truth and Objective reality, which isn't conflict resolution or problem solving, but force and manipulation. It's not a logical exercise to take part in and there's no benefit long term in forcing someone to accept your particular lie as reality.

Now we're ready to move into Processing.

Processing Steps Summarized

The entire thrust of Gateway #2 or Processing is to take the vent and elevate it into a higher format of perception. It's time to look at the vent, the triggers, the experience we're having from the perspective of the Higher Self.

The following steps summarize the Processing exercise.

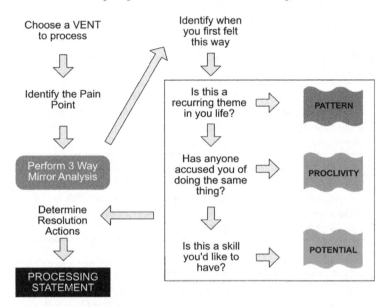

Processing Steps
STEP 1: Complete the Venting Exercise for whatever vent I wish to process. NOTE: I must be in a place of relative peace around what I was triggered about. If I still have anger or anxiety around my trigger, go back and do additional venting. To Process, I should be at a level 2 or below, emotionally.
STEP 2: Review My Trigger and what I articulated during the vent to clearly identify the pain point/s at the root of the trigger. The pain point is the essence of what triggered you, the specific thing/s that stands out and caused emotionality.
STEP 3: Take the pain point into the 3-Way Mirror process.
3-Way Mirror Steps:

STEP 3A: Ask This Question Within: What is the first time I felt triggered in a similar way in the past? Meaning, is this something you seem to experience over and over again with different people and in different situations. If I have felt a similar way in the past, I may have uncovered a PATTERN reflection that needs further analysis and understanding through the 3-Way Mirror process. If I don't find a pain point I have experienced before, move to STEP 3b of the 3-Way Mirror Steps.

STEP 3B: Ask This Question Within: Has anyone ever accused me of doing something similar or has anyone been triggered by me in a similar way that I was triggered? If YES, what you observed and were triggered by is a PROCLIVITY — Go to STEP 4. If NO, go to 3C.

STEP 3C: Ask This Question Within: Would I like to have a similar skill, demeanor, or ability of the person who triggered me? Would I like to be similar in character as the person who triggered me? Would I like to do what they do? If YES, what you observed and were triggered by was a POTENTIAL. Go to STEP 4.

End 3-Way Mirror Steps

STEP 4: Work out a plan for resolving the part of me that is triggered. I now know the source of the trigger — Pattern, Proclivity, or Potential — I can begin to resolve it within myself. If I found the source of the trigger inside of the 3-Way Mirror process then I can work to resolve the subconscious, reflexive behavior pattern through the tools designed for that work (i.e., meditation, LACING™, EFT, affirmations, etc.). If the trigger isn't a reflection (i.e., I answered NO to all three sub headers in STEP 3), then I can simply practice a new skill and develop my character in a way that transcends the cultural beliefs and character limitations I currently possess. Go to STEP 5.

STEP 5: Write or speak a Processing statement, indicating my understanding of the source of the trigger I experienced. This statement should reflect my findings from the 3-Way Mirror process. If you answered NO to all of the 3-Way Mirror process questions, then assume your trigger is POTENTIAL-based for the sake of writing your Processing statement.

Processing Steps in Detail

We only move into STEP 1 once we've completed our venting exercise. The goal of venting is to allow our Ego to be heard and to physically release the tension we're otherwise storing in our body. This is important for two reasons: (1) energy (in the form of tension and anxiety) is difficult to store in the body without it doing damage to us mentally and physically; thus, we need to remove it expeditiously when we sense its presence, and (2) we can't really be in our Higher Self when we carry tension because that tension affects our consciousness and lowers our cognitive ability, which ultimately keeps us in the Animal state of consciousness. Processing is a form of Higher Self expression through Ego; thus, it requires our body and mind to be somewhat free of the tension we typically experience during a triggering event.

However, another important consideration here in STEP 1 is for us to be ready to process. Meaning, we need to be in a good place mentally, emotionally, and especially spiritually in order to process. We need to be in the right frame of mind in order to objectively look at our traumas. It's not easy to objectively look at people we feel have wronged us (i.e., villains). It's not easy to come out of victim mode when we have identified there for decades. It's not easy to look at others as anything beyond *the villain* when we feel that's exactly who they are. What's even more difficult is to sift through all the excuses we've given ourselves for why we're not better or happier or further along in life and acknowledge we have some unhealed traumas that have created habits and expectations of mediocrity. Are we really ready to release our excuses and move into personal responsibility and accountability? Are we really willing to see the scenario from the Higher Self perspective? Are we ready to look objectively at all things, experiences, and people, including those who appeared to have caused pain? I know we may say "Yes" to these questions, but execution of Processing is easier said than done. Pain can cloud our judgment as we generally have been taught to look at life from outside the Progressive Love™ tenets.

- No Shame, No Blame
- No Victims, No Villains
- No Cop Outs, No Drop Outs
- The Purpose Is Growth, The Benefit is Love
- I Create My Life

Being objective about where our pain and conditionings are sourced is very delicate work and requires a clear mind. For this reason, it's recommended that we only Process when we're truly ready. Again, being ready to process means we're at a level 2 or below in terms of emotionality around the original trigger. We must choose to stay in vent until the tension subsides enough to Process.

The 3-Way Mirror Exercise

In processing our deepest triggers, those we took note of as we vented, we'll find that we're usually triggered by our own reflection of self in others. What is a reflection? A reflection is a view of oneself outside oneself, a view of self reflected from others. When we look out into the world, what are we looking at? We're looking at ourselves. How do we know this? It's simple to see that we're always looking at reflections of ourselves in others when we begin to note what triggers us about others.

The 3-Way Mirror (3WM) is a system that fits inside the UPLVL Communication™ format seamlessly. The 3WM shows us how our own thoughts, feelings, attitudes, stories and ideals are creating everyone around us to be only what we ourselves are. It's simple to note how incredibly our triggers resemble the very thoughts we think daily. The 3WM helps us to see how our own thoughts are literally creating the experiences we have on a regular basis. To prove the 3WM system and to show how it works, we'll look at a few examples.

The question we ask when processing a vent is: How am I creating this?

The answer is, we're creating through one of three kinds of reflections, primarily:

- Patterns
- Potentials
- Proclivities

A Patterns Reflection shows us thoughts we've been thinking for a number of years, maybe since youth. When we see our own Patterns reflected in another, we're seeing what we believe to be true. Thus, we're seeing our own beliefs reflected back to us. A Pattern is formulated in youth, and we hold onto the idea for many years until we are triggered enough to work on it. One Pattern we might hold is beliefs about men. Maybe our father was emotionally distant; thus, we believe men, in general, are emotionally distant.

When we're in a scenario where men are behaving in emotionally distant ways, we find ourselves becoming triggered by this behavior. Why? The subconscious mind is showing us something we believe, deeply, but aren't at peace within. We don't like that we believe this is true. Thus, we become triggered by the reflection or projection of this thought onto the scenario at hand. In essence, we're creating the scenario by holding onto the thought that men are emotionally distant. If we didn't believe that men were emotionally distant, we wouldn't have attracted this scenario that proves out thought correct.

Pattern Reflections are really prevalent in cultures where dysfunction between youth and their parents is a recurring theme. Whatever traumas you experienced in youth generally become your Patterns. We'll continue to see repeating versions of the stories we learned from our parents and how they were with us. We'll see the repeating Patterns in all of our relationships until we become aware of the Patterns and shift the stories beneath them.

Potentials reflections are not about the past at all; they're truly about the future. A Potentials reflection shows us, in another, the very attributes we want to achieve. We look out into the world and see the projection or reflection of our "future selves" when we see behaviors in others we adore and love. We might even become triggered when we see a person reflecting our Potentials if they've already achieved what we want such as money, power, love, or spirituality.

When we're triggered by a person reflecting our Potential, we call this a Potentials Reflection. By identifying how this person reflects a trait we have yet to discover and master, we can begin to process a vent by understanding how we created this person. We created this person to show us the part of yourself that's empowered to do what we want to do, and do it well! But why would this trigger us? Potentials Reflections usually trigger us because they make us aware that we still have work to do.

A Proclivities Reflection is a direct, one-to-one version of something we're doing, have done, or continue to struggle with in the present. One of our clients came to us with a story about how her messy husband leaves his messy socks on the floor daily. What she didn't see is that her husband was a direct, one-to-one reflection of her own clutter, except she didn't leave socks about; she left unfinished work at her office and led a cluttered career life. While she hated the fact that her husband wouldn't pick up, organize, and systematize his socks, she had yet to organize and confront her own career messes. So, she was seeing a reflection of her own similar attribute, albeit her show of messy behavior wasn't at home, but at the office.

So, it's always either a Pattern, Potential, or Proclivity that we're observing when we look out into the world at others. Once we can begin to recognize these kinds of reflections of our thoughts and personal worlds onto others, we can then process any vent and understand the answer to the quintessential question: *How Am I Creating This?*

Analyzing the Original Vent and Interlocked Trigger

Once we've moved past the venting exercise, we can go back to the trigger and analyze exactly what triggered us. This is critical because there's usually one specific thing that is the pain point, but it might not be so obvious. For example, if we're triggered by our partner cheating on us, we may interpret the pain point as our partner breaking their agreement when the real pain point may be anxiety around perceived rejection or not feeling we're lovable. Triggers aren't as obvious as they may seem; thus, we need to take the time to analyze them carefully. Take as much time as needed to come to the absolute truth of why we felt the way we did before we go into further processing.

Identifying the real pain point is done by asking these questions:

- What bothers me most about what I have vented about?
- What is the worst feeling I experience in this situation?

123

- What is the worst thing about this situation?
- What really bothers me about the situation I just vented about?

After we've clearly identified the pain point, we can move into STEP 3 and the 3-Way Mirror exercise to see exactly why this pain point exists. Understanding why we feel the way we feel is just as important as understanding what we're feeling. It's how we learn about ourselves and ultimately address the source of the trigger. The foundation for our feelings is in our personal stories we've told ourselves or accepted about life. These stories were built from a combination of nature and nurture influence. It's the combination of our personal make-up as illustrated by our mental and emotional coding given to us at birth and what we've adopted culturally from those around us. Are our triggers inherent parts of our character, bestowed upon us from birth? If so, we know it's a matter of developing the character traits that are implicitly weak in our natal character. If, however, our triggers are a result of a cultural learning from childhood, we know we can address the lie by rewriting the narrative on how to feel and behave in certain situations. This is the key to character development, growth, and change for us as human beings.

In STEP 3a, we ask the question if we've felt triggered in a similar way before in the past. It may not be the same exact people or events who triggered us, but the same feelings seem to be recurring intermittently throughout our lives. Again, this level of analysis takes a level of honesty and introspection that comes with practice. Have I felt this way before in another situation? How often have I felt this way? What were the similarities of events that took place to cause me to feel that way?

If we find that we feel this feeling often, and that it has occurred before, repeatedly, it could be the result of a trauma that we've experienced at an earlier age, often childhood. In this case, the trauma becomes a memory, which manifests itself intermittently over our lifetime. This happens because our lives unfold and are created based on subconscious projections. Meaning, what we expect to happen is what will actually happen. We can only see the reality we understand. This is why two people can live in the same environment and one person sees depression and poverty and the other sees opportunity and prosperity. This occurs because one has been trained to have a poverty consciousness and always see the worst in people and the world and the other person has been trained to have prosperity consciousness and always looks for opportunity no matter where they are. When we experience the same triggers over and over again based on a past trauma, we call those PATTERN reflections.

In STEP 3b, we move to determine if we display behavior that matches the reflection we're seeing in the person or event that has triggered us. The question is meant to determine if we do the exact same thing we vented about, which is quite possible because we all possess qualities about ourselves that we're not particularly fond of or, in some cases, we downright despise. It's true that we don't feel good when we exercise those qualities, but it can be especially annoying when we see those same qualities in other people. In this case, it means a part of us desperately wants to get beyond our current mode of functioning and elevate into something we can be proud of, which usually means, a new behavior reflecting a higher potential. A direct reflection is called a PROCLIVITY. It's when we do the same thing that we observed and were subsequently triggered by.

In STEP 3c we ask ourselves if we'd secretly desire to be like the people who triggered us. Meaning, we find that when people have achieved a certain level of proficiency in an area that we haven't yet, it can be bothersome to observe them enjoying the benefits of having that skill. We see similar behavior when it comes to people who have monetary wealth versus those who don't where there can be resentment toward those who have it. In this case, we're talking about a specific ability that we'd like to have. This is called a POTENTIALS reflection.

STEP 4 is about putting together a plan of action to resolve the trigger by eliminating the internal pain point. How to do that is beyond the scope of this book, but we essentially utilize tools like LACING™ and meditation to rewrite the stories we've accepted as truth to be in our favor. Regardless of your specific strategy for resolving your pain point, you can move to STEP 5, which is stating clearly what the trigger is and why you have it and that you realize the trigger isn't your truth. This step is the PROCESSING part of the exercise. Ideally, we make these Processing statements to a Witness, but it's not mandatory to do so. The important thing is that we're clear on where the trigger is coming from so that we have a fighting chance to change it going forward. The Witness can certainly be the same person who witnessed the vent, which is beneficial because they'll be the ones who most appreciate us going full circle from venting to processing. They also have the background information because they were there to witness the vent; thus, they'll have a better chance to understand the processing work.

Processing Case Studies

We'll continue with the same case studies from our venting exercises done in Gateway #1. It may be helpful to review the each of these case studies in the Venting section as a refresher.

Case Study #1: In this example, a husband is mad that his wife didn't tell him that she used to date one of his friends from college. He found out through another mutual friend at a party just last night and they've been married for twelve years.

Now that we've vented, we can move to processing. In STEP 1, the husband is judging that he's in a place of relative peace around the situation. He can now move to STEP 2 to find the root of what he's feeling. The question to ask is "What exactly is agitating me?" In this case, the husband can go through the exercise of analyzing what he's feeling. Is it embarrassment, jealousy, insecurity, or betrayal? Is it disappointment? All of these seem to fit to a degree, but let's say that insecurity feels the strongest. Now we'll take the pain point of insecurity into the 3-Way Mirror analysis exercises.

STEP 3a asks when was the first time we felt these emotions and triggers. In this case, the husband can remember a few scenarios: (a) one time when he was in college and really liked this girl, but she ended up choosing his friend instead and (b) when he was a child and his mother bought a toy car and toy plane for him and his brother, but gave the plane to his brother when that's the toy he really wanted. He remembers crying about it for an hour, but the mother still giving him the toy car. On top of that, his brother teased him about it for weeks afterwards.

Those are two possible scenarios that are related to the first time he felt triggers of insecurity. As the husband digs deeper, he remembers how his father left his mother when he was seven years old and he felt rejected as a result of that. What made matters worse was the mother moved another man into the house who eventually became his stepfather and she would always prioritize the stepfather over him and his brother. She never had time for them, but always seemed to be available for whatever the stepfather wanted. This felt like rejection and made him feel insecure about his worth as a child. Both the mother and father seemingly rejected him for someone else. After the divorce and his mother's remarriage, he began to have issues in school and feeling extra sensitive about being left out of the cool friend cliques. When he started dating, he noticed feelings of jealousy about who his girlfriends had been with before him and would sometimes suspect them of cheating without any real evidence. Overall, he can remember a general feeling of insecurity that existed just below the surface for most of his life.

In this case, he decides that insecurity is the primary pain point he's dealing with regarding this trigger. The other emotions are also important and they can be revisited in another processing session. Moreover this is a PATTERN because it has been a recurring theme in his life.

This seems to be very solid analysis for STEP 3a, so now we move to STEPS 3b-3c and ask specific questions to pinpoint the reflection. In STEP 3b the question is whether we do the same thing to others that we get triggered about when done to us. The husband reflected on whether he withheld information from his wife or others that they would probably want to know or that he thought might be too sensitive for them to know. The answer to that question is YES. He didn't tell his wife that he had coffee with a young lady he met while in the mall one day. Nothing happened with her, but he felt his wife would think so if he told her the truth. So, we've identified a PROCLIVITY.

STEP 3c asks if we would actually want to have the skill or disposition to do what was done to us. In this case, would we like the ability to withhold telling the truth about information our loved ones would want to know. In this case, the husband assesses that he already has the ability to withhold key information from people he's close too; thus, this isn't something he feels he needs to develop. So, the answer is NO; therefore, this reflection isn't a POTENTIAL.

The result of our 3-Way Mirror analysis is the trigger was sourced by a both a PROCLIVITY and PATTERN reflection. In other words, this is why the husband was triggered because it's reflecting a part of himself that hasn't healed from a childhood trauma. It also stems from a current behavior he possesses that he's not proud of and even feels guilty about.

In STEP 4, we can determine a resolution to heal this past trauma, which will cause the trigger to disappear. The details of which tools are available and how to apply them are beyond the scope of this work; however, processes like LACING™, hypnotherapy, mediation, ritual and ceremony work, plant medicine work, etc. are just a few that can be applied.

To heal the PROCLIVITY reflection, the husband must simply become more understanding and accepting of his own ability to withhold the truth and thus, he won't be as bothered when others do the same.

Now, let's take some time in STEP 5 to write our Processing Statement, which will essentially summarize our analysis of the source of the trigger. The processing statement may look as follows and can be read to the person who witnessed the original vent, shared with another Witness, or kept to yourself.

"All my life I've felt as though people were going to choose others over me. I've felt as though I was never really a priority and that other people's feelings, wants, and desires would always come before mine. I remember this starting when I was a child and perceiving that my mother would prioritize my brother over me. It always felt like he got exactly what he wanted, but what I wanted wasn't as important. I might get what I wanted as long as he was taken care of first. I just remember feeling this way from an early age. Looking back at it, I perceived it wrong. My mother was just trying to do the best she could to raise us and keep us happy. "When my father left, it reinforced this sense of insecurity I already had. It seemed like not only my mother would make me less of a priority, but also my father. I guess this is why it hurt so bad. I guess you represented my mother subconsciously and my best friend represented my father. You all seemed to prioritize one another over me. Like my feelings and opinions didn't matter.

"I realize now that this is a story I tell myself and project onto others. I realize no one is doing anything to me. However, I do take things personally when they match my story of insecurity I developed as a child. I'm glad I was able to see this so clearly. This is definitely a PATTERN that I need to resolve quickly."

The processing statement is a succinct summary of where the trigger was sourced from. It's the beginning of acknowledging healing within yourself as well as letting others know you're on the healing journey as well.

End of Processing Analysis

NOTE: If the Processing Statement is read to a Witness, the Witness is free to ask questions to support getting deeper at the truth.

Case Study #2: In this example, a wife suspects that her husband has cheated on her. The wife's friend sent her a picture of the husband out with another woman and being intimate with her (i.e., holding hands and kissing).

Now that venting has been completed and the wife has found relative peace in the situation (STEP 1), she can move to STEP 2. Our first task is to identify the pain point. In this case, we need to be extra vigilant because there are so many options for what could be the source of hurt. Here are some possibilities:

- The embarrassment that her friend saw her husband out with another woman and had to tell her about it. It's one thing for her husband to cheat on her, but another for her to find out after her friend. There's additional embarrassment in the fact that the cheating can't be spun as something else. If the wife would have found out first then she could tell herself whatever story she wanted too, but now the narrative is controlled by someone outside of her. In addition, it's likely that her friend will tell their other mutual friends at some point if it hasn't already happened. This adds extra pressure for the wife to take "socially expected" action around the cheating event.

- The hurt that what she thought she had with her husband is revealed to be a lie. She thought they were in love and sexually exclusive with one another. She knew that she was deeply in love with him and loved what they had built together thus far and believed he felt the same way. To find out he didn't cherish what they had is painful.

- A feeling of being disrespected by the husband in two ways: (1) that he would be so sloppy as to appear in a public place with another woman when people in the community know he's married and (2) that he would dare betray his vows and take her so lightly as to be with another woman. What is this saying about her? Did he even think about how this could affect her if it got out into the public? Did he even consider her feelings before doing this?

- She feels a level of foolishness for marrying him in the first place when she had her suspicions that he wasn't a solid man to begin with. Why didn't she trust her gut? Especially, as he wasn't even the one whom she loved the most when she agreed to marry him. She honestly felt like she was dating down to be with him. Some of her friends even questioned why she was with him, but she assured them that he was a good guy.

- She feels insecure that maybe there's something wrong with her. Is the sex not good enough? Is she gaining weight? Is she no longer attractive? Maybe she never bounced back from having children or maybe he can feel she's not as into sex right now. Thoughts of *there must be a reason why he would cheat* come up for her. Maybe I'm just not a good wife to my husband.
- A feeling of acute anger about his actions.

After reviewing all the possibilities, she decides that the feeling of disrespect stands out the strongest and is the primary pain point. It doesn't mean the other alternatives aren't also viable pain points, but she's focusing on what stands out the strongest as a place to begin the processing work.

Next we move into our 3-Way Mirror analysis work. STEP 3a asks when was the first time she can remember feeling disrespected. There were a few memories that came to mind for her:

- She's had two boyfriends cheat on her in the past before, and, in both of those cases, she felt disrespected. The first time was a boyfriend in high school. He was her first experience with love, and it hurt badly when he cheated on her with a girl from the cheerleading team. The second took place in college with a man she thought she was going to marry after graduation, but he was a serial cheater and had sex with numerous women while they were together. What made it so bad was he was having sex with other girls on campus and a lot people knew about it before she did.
- There was a time at work when her boss recognized a coworker for their efforts on a joint project, but didn't recognize her.

This was especially hurtful because she put in the most work to get the project done.

- Another memory brought her back to her mother spanking her for drawing on the wall at their home. She felt like she hadn't done anything wrong and was happy about the drawing, but her mother was furious. She remembers getting in trouble and her mother talking about her for months afterwards. In hindsight, she realized she shouldn't have drawn on the wall, but at the time when it happened, she didn't see any issue and prior to that her mother had always encouraged her to draw and be creative. The incident felt like a contradiction and slap in the face.

These were her earliest memories of feeling a kind of disrespect. All of these memories are valid examples of past feelings of disrespect. **As a general rule, we go back to the earliest as the possible source for where our story around disrespect was written.** In this case, it would be getting in trouble for writing on the wall as a child. Because we have a solid memory of this happening in the past, we're leaning toward the reflection being either a PROCLIVITY or a PATTERN.

Next we ask the question in STEP 3a if feeling disrespected is a recurring theme in her life. As she has identified above, it is. She remembered numerous examples throughout her life when she had felt disrespected in one way or another including in relationships with men. So we've confirmed a PATTERN reflection.

Next we ask the question in STEP 3b if she's ever been the trigger of someone else feeling disrespected. After careful thought, she determines the answer is NO. She had never gotten complaints from others that she disrespected them.

In STEP 3c we ask if she desires to have the ability to live her life the way she wants even if others determine her actions to be disrespectful. After careful analysis, she determines the answer is NO. She feels she is living her authentic life right now and doesn't need to do anything further to feel more fulfilled.

In STEP 4 we put together an action plan to eradicate the feelings of disrespect she feels when cheated on or in any other scenario. Again, this is where tools like meditation, LACING™, hypnotherapy, coaching, working with subliminal audios, etc. would come into the picture.

In STEP 5 she puts together a Processing Statement that explains the entire source and reason for the trigger and emotional response to the cheating. Here's how it might look:

"This is my processing statement for my trigger about my husband cheating on me with another woman. After looking at the situation closely, I pinpointed that my Ego felt disrespected by his actions. When my girlfriend sent me the pictures of him out with another woman, it felt like a slap in the face. It felt like he knew better but purposefully decided to hurt me. From my Ego's standpoint, that counts as disrespect. It's a disregard for me, the deepest part of who I am.

"When I think back to the first time I felt the feeling of disrespect, it was when my mother spanked me for drawing with crayons on the walls in our home. She had so often told me I was an artist and was special and would do great things when I grew up. She bought me crayons and coloring books and I really felt like I was loved and respected even as a child. But when she yelled at me and punished me for drawing, my inner child felt angry as if I had been lied to and betrayed. My inner child felt as if she had been disrespected by my mother. This feeling only intensified over the following weeks as she continued to mention it to family and friends and threaten me with further punishment if I ever did it again. I realize at this point in my life that whenever someone does something to signal that I'm not important, my inner child gets angry and offended. It's a deep hurt that brings me back to that childhood experience and all other similar experiences of disrespect.

"After further analysis, I realize that my husband cheating on me is a similar experience because marriage, loyalty, and family are so very important to me. Honestly, they have become my personal identity to the point where I haven't taken the time to refind myself. It was the same thing with the drawing as a child where my artistry was what I identified with. This is the source of my trigger around my husband cheating, and, although I'm totally against what he did, it's clear that my emotions went way deeper than what's healthy for me.

"Upon doing the 3-Way Mirror analysis, I realized that this is a PATTERN for me. It keeps coming up in different ways at different times throughout my life. It's come up before when two of my ex-boyfriends cheated on me and it's come up at a previous job as well when I felt overlooked for proper credit on a project I had worked exceptionally hard on. This concludes my processing."

This processing statement can be shared with her husband or other loved ones who know the situation or anyone she feels close too. It should be noted that no explicit action is being stated with this processing. It's unknown whether she'll stay in the marriage, leave the marriage, open the marriage, or anything in between. The processing is strictly about getting to the source of why she was triggered so intensely.

There's always the question of whether the pain point analysis is actually right or not. What happens if there's an error with identifying the correct pain point? Well, the good news is that, either way, we've identified something that needs to be processed and worked through. Either way, we've identified a trauma from earlier in our lives that could use some attention and healing. For this reason, no one should feel anxiety over pinpointing the exact pain point. It's not super critical to get it one-hundred percent right. In addition, if we do choose the wrong pain point, the trigger will continue to come up and we can keep working on finding the source. So, it's never a missed opportunity.

End of Processing Analysis

Case Study #3: In this example, someone has been passed up for promotion for the third time by someone they feel isn't as skilled or deserving as them. In this specific example, we're going to assume the employees at the company are trained in the UPLVL Communication™ protocols; thus, the employee has vented to their supervisor.

Now that we have completed the venting exercise for this particular trigger, we can move to STEP 2 and determine what the pain point is. Here are some of the feelings that seem to be related to this trigger: (1) A feeling of being minimize and marginalized, (2) feeling unappreciated, (3) anger and resentment, and (4) feeling unapologetic.

Based on these examples, the Employee can say that the dominant emotion is actually anger so she'll move into STEP 3 and process it.

In STEP 3a we can look at memories of when the Employee has felt this way in the past.

- "When I was younger, I remember playing sports and my coach saying that I wasn't assertive enough on the field. He said I cared too much about making sure others were involved and, for that reason, I couldn't be team captain. He gave that honor to someone else. At that time, I felt like I was passed up. I was angry to the point where all I could see was red after I was passed up for captain."

- "I remember my sister and I baking a cake for Thanksgiving when we were children. It came out really well. When our aunts and uncles asked us who made the cake, my mother said it was my sister's project and I helped out. The truth was it was my idea to make the cake, but I was fine giving my sister credit and being in the background. Again, the feeling I had here was a deep anger that boiled beneath the surface."

In addition, based on these memories, she can say that what triggers her is the propensity to not speak up for herself when she deserves credit. It's her tendency to play the background and not assert herself more in life.

In STEP 3a, we're seeing if there is a PATTERN in some way at play here. This kind of trigger is a recurring theme, but it's not necessarily a PATTERN because the truth is she wants to be more assertive in her life. This isn't something she's experiencing because of a past trauma, but rather something she'd like to get better at. It's essentially a character deficiency that's been plaguing the Employee her entire life. So we'll say NO to the PATTERN reflection here.

She's never been accused of passing up others in any way, so there's no PROCLIVITY here for STEP 3b.

Per her initial analysis, she can see there is some POTENTIAL reflection at work here. It's not that she wants to pass others up when they are deserving of credit, but she needs to be more selfish and assertive and put herself first just like her coworkers do. They aren't advocating for her to get promoted first. They are advocating for themselves. She needs to be more like that in her life as well, so a definite POTENTIAL has been identified in STEP 3C.

In STEP 4, we can work out a plan for resolution of the trigger and emotion. In this case, hypnotherapy and confidence training may do the trick.

Now that we're clear on where the trigger is coming from, we can write our Processing Statement.

"All of my life, I've wanted to achieve great things. I've wanted to excel in so many ways, but I've always found myself coming up short of my own expectations. I'm clear now that a part of me wasn't ready to be in the spotlight but, instead, just wanted to play the background and not receive any credit.

"Every time I see someone else get the credit they deserve, I get triggered. Every time I see someone putting their self first, especially at my expense, I get triggered and angry. Why? Because I realize I need to do this for myself. This is definitely a POTENTIAL I'd like to realize in my life."

End of Processing Analysis

Case Study #4: In this example a relationship coach is feeling that her friend is forcing free coaching sessions on her by coming to the house and discussing her relationship life. This friend has purchased coaching from her before in the past, but lately has seemingly been trying to get free coaching by leveraging her access via their friendship.

Now that we've completed the venting exercise for this trigger, we can move to processing. In STEP 2, we're determining what the specific pain point is around the trigger we've experienced. Here are some possibilities:

- Feeling used and taken advantage of by people close to her
- Not feeling valued for one's skills and accomplishments
- Feeling disrespected

- Not feeling loved by those close to her
- Feeling like a doormat for others to walk over
- Not feeling worthy of getting paid what she's worth

After careful consideration of the possible pain points, it became abundantly clear that the fear of not being paid and valued for one's worth is the primary pain point. It's essentially a combination of the second and last listed pain point.

We can now move to STEP 3 and our 3-Way Mirror analysis. In STEP 3a, we ask the first time we've felt this same trigger before. Here is what she came up with as the possibilities:

- Early in her coaching practice, she only coached family and friends and didn't charge any money. She only received donations. This felt great at first, but then started to feel like exploitation because the appreciation wasn't being expressed.
- When she was dating her boyfriend in college, she used to clean his apartment, do his laundry, and cook for him regularly. Initially, she enjoyed doing this and it was her idea and suggestion to do it, but over time, she didn't see equal return coming from her boyfriend. She started to feel used and that she should be receiving more from a relationship.

The boyfriend scenario, although not directly related, seemed to resonate the most as the first trigger of this kind. It's the act of feeling as though you're being taken advantage of by those who are close to you. They leverage their position and access to you in order to extract a service or benefit. Thus, the college boyfriend example is the first time this trigger was experienced.

We need to ask if this is a pattern for us. Does this type of thing seem to happen over and over? The answer is YES it does, but it's not overly rampant. However, we'll say YES for a PATTERN reflection.

In STEP 3b we ask if we've ever been accused of doing the same thing as we're accusing our friend of and the answer is YES, sometimes. It doesn't feel rampant and no one has ever really had a major issue around it, but it has occurred so we'll say there is a PROCLIVITY reflection at work here.

Next, in STEP 3c we need to ask if we need to adopt this type of behavior where we leverage ourselves and our position to get what we want. In truth, this is an area of development that needs to be improved upon. They underutilize their position with others. For example, with her ex-boyfriend, she felt that they could have actually worked things out if she would have asked him for what she wanted instead of just expecting him to give it to her. She wanted more time, love, touch, and to do more special things together, but never asked him for it and, instead, simply resented him not giving it. So we definitely have a POTENTIALS reflection here.

So the primary reflection is a POTENTIAL reflection with some PATTERN and PROCLIVITY as well. In STEP 4 we can put a plan of action together to address the fact that she needs to learn to ask for what she wants. This could be a combination of coaching and some subliminal audio work.

In STEP 5 we can put together a processing statement that summarizes our awareness of where the trigger came from and exactly what it is.

"All my life I've been the nice girl. I've been the one to consider everyone else's feelings, wants, needs, and desires over my own. It's gotten me a good reputation that's allowed me to enter spaces where I otherwise wouldn't have been invited into. I think this is primarily because people saw me as safe and not a threat to them, but I'm realizing that's not an accurate statement. In reality, they saw me as someone who offered low cost value to them. Meaning, I never demanded my worth while simultaneously giving them everything I had. I was cheap, like a slave or servant. What's worse is that this demeanor allowed me to advance in life in so many ways. Boyfriends would use me because there was so much benefit for them because I didn't ask for anything. I did expect something, though, but just seemed to always be disappointed when I didn't get it.

"The same thing happened at work where I would always be hired and promoted, but not necessarily paid my worth. This is what I'm seeing in the POTENTIALS reflection of my friend who wants free coaching from me: the ability of someone to actually ask for what they want and feel as though that's okay because they have the relationship. What are connections for if you're not willing to leverage them? I need to do better.

"So, I totally see why I'm triggered by my friend asking me for free coaching because I need to learn to do the same thing."

End of Processing Analysis

Gateway #3 — OWNERSHIP

The primary Progressive Love™ tenet that governs the entire UPLVL Communication™ protocol and everything we do in life is "I Create My Life. Who creates it? We do. Do we collectively create our lives? No. I completely create mine and you completely create yours. What about when we both have an argument? We still didn't cocreate that reality. I one-hundred percent created my reality and experience and you one-hundred percent created your reality and experience. That's just the reality of it. When we analyze it deeper, we see that how each person shows up in that argument is subject to interpretation. One person could be saying they were the voice of reason when that contradicts the perceptions of the other. Even though we were both there, we'll rarely agree on how each of us presented ourselves. We'll have different perceptions of what even happened when we came together where one person says it was an argument and the other says it was a discussion. In other words, two people can experience the same exact situation differently. So, no, it's never a joint creation, but always a complete creation for each person involved. This understanding spares us the fruitless pursuit of attempting to determine what percentage blame to place on each person.

Another way to say "I Create My Life" is to say — I Own My Creation, which brings us to gateway #4 — Ownership.

What are we taking ownership of? The fact that I've one-hundred percent created the situation that triggered me and brought out this uncomfortable emotion. How did I create it? I created it based on my "story," which defines who I am, how I expect to feel in certain situations, how I expect people to show up in my life, and all my perceptions. Our stories literally define everything about us, not just our interaction with people. Things like our relationship to money, health, family, children, travel, how we dress, exercise, hobbies, career, and the list goes on. Remember — No one is doing anything to us. They're simply acting out their lives based on their stories; however, at times, your story will bring you into my life and our individual stories will define the quality of our interaction together.

We illuminated this in part during our Processing exercise in which we found out the source of our feelings comes from us seeing a part of ourselves in other people as either a Potential, Proclivity, or Pattern reflection. Seeing a part of ourselves that we haven't resolved yet brings about an emotional response that tends to be uncomfortable (i.e., trigger). So it's not what the person did per se, but rather our story about that specific action we're responding too. It could have been anyone who did the same thing and we would have had the same reaction to it.

No Apology

This is how we get to a place of taking one-hundred percent ownership of our lives, feelings, and perceptions. But here's the thing — if we're all one-hundred percent responsible for our creation, then there's no need to apologize when someone is triggered by our actions. Sure, you can apologize, but what are we really apologizing for? What's an apology really about anyway? If we're apologizing for making someone feel a certain emotion, then that apology is misplaced. We're in no position to take responsibility for someone else's feelings because how they feel is completely out of our control. If you'd like to apologize for not doing something you said you'd do or for not meeting your own personal expectations, then you're in a better position for that. But it doesn't make sense to take responsibility for someone else's emotional responses. It wasn't your fault — No Shame. Even in a scenario where you know the person gets triggered whenever you do or say a particular thing, it's still not your fault. Now, if you make a promise to yourself to make a change for your own personal development and you want to acknowledge (take ownership) of the Animal within you having the upper hand in preventing you from making the change, then fine, but that's a different thing entirely.

"I apologize that my Animal nature still has me desire comfort over creating new habits and patterns in my life. I acknowledge the Animal part of myself is fully active, but I'm slowly learning to tame that part of myself."

"I apologize for being late. I know I said I'd be here by noon, but I was in my Ego earlier and justified my lateness by saying I deserve to have more time to myself. That Ego perspective got in the way of me getting ready on time."

These types of apologies make sense because they take full ownership for how we created our lives. We're acknowledging a part of ourselves that is contradicting a principle we claim to want to embody. Let's look at the old paradigm ways of apologizing to others where we take full responsibility for how the other person feels while simultaneously taking on all the guilt and shame upon ourselves.

"I'm sorry I made you feel bad today. I can be such an asshole sometimes. I promise, I'll never do that again."

"I really screwed up this time. I broke your heart again, and I feel horrible about it. Please forgive me."

In these examples, the person apologizing has succeeded in doing three things:

- Taking full responsibility for the other person's feelings, emotions, and triggers
- Taking on full blame while also shaming their self
- Either outright promising or implying that they'll never do the triggering behavior again

This is problematic because it creates more issues than it solves. We've already got a situation where people are triggered and emotional, which means there's some unresolved childhood traumas that haven't been addressed. Why make the situation worse by taking responsibility for someone else's childhood traumas? Why make it worse by saying things that will prevent them from looking within at the source of their triggers? What's even worse here is that the person apologizing ends up feeling bad about how they made the other person feel, which means now they take on the emotional burden whenever the person is triggered the same way in the future regardless of who triggered them. Every time they're triggered the emotions of guilt come back because they feel partly responsible. Why? Maybe they feel their actions caused the issue to begin with, not knowing this is a part of that person's story. It's just not necessary to take on these kinds of burdens. Lastly, one of the most difficult things we can do is stick to our word when it goes against our established patterns and modes of behavior. We can't promise someone we'll never make them angry when we've been making people angry since our infancy. We can't promise someone that we'll eat right or exercise regularly when that hasn't been our proclivity to this point in our lives. So why set ourselves up for failure when we don't have to?

Let's take ownership for our feelings and responses. Let's take ownership of our stories and perceptions so that we have a fighting chance to change them in our favor. Ask yourself — do you really want your emotional health and stability to be in the hands of another person. Do you really want the emotions of anger, depression, guilt, doubt, and happiness to be the result of what others do versus what you want for yourself? This is why we must Process. This is why we must take ownership of our own emotions; otherwise, we're like lost ships at sea just being tossed based on the flow of events and other people's words and actions. Ownership is empowerment and empowerment is the only way to shape our lives.

How to Take Ownership

The way we take ownership for our lives and actions is the same way we vent and process. We set container and acknowledge who we are and that we've created the scenario that triggered us. In that very moment, we've taken our power back and put ourselves in the driver's seat.

We all have the option to take ownership with just ourselves or with a Witness. Setting container can look as follows.

Owner: "Are you willing to hear me take ownership for the situation I created last week?"

Witness: "Yes, I am."

Owner: "I'd like to acknowledge that I take one-hundred percent responsibility for creating that situation last week. I've vented and processed and understand that I am the sole creator of everything I experienced. Thank you for holding space for me."

Witness: "You're welcome."

That's it. Short and sweet and to the point. No long soliloquy needed. Again, you don't need a Witness for this because you can just acknowledge your creation to yourself; however, having a Witness has its advantages too because it further solidifies that you have no fear or hang-ups around taking full responsibility by declaring this in front of others. To that point, if you've had a situation with someone and they vented and processed, feel free to get into Witness mode and approach them about taking ownership. This is an unsolicited approach by the Witness to the person taking ownership. Here's an example.

Witness: "Hi. I was wondering if you were ready to take ownership about the situation that happened last week. If so, I'm here to Witness you stepping into ownership."

Owner: "Thanks for asking. Yes, I'm ready to take ownership. I'd like to acknowledge that I take one-hundred percent responsibility for creating that situation last week. I've vented and processed and understand that I am the sole creator of everything I experienced. Thank you for holding space for me."

Witness: "You're welcome."

This is how we support each other in our growth pursuits. Again, approaching someone in this way assumes they have done their venting and processing work, as they are both prerequisites to taking ownership. You can't take ownership if you haven't vented and allowed the Animal to be heard. You can't take ownership if you haven't processed to identify where the source of the trigger and emotions is coming from.

Action Plan

There's one more aspect to ownership that we need to address and that's the action we're going to take to adjust our story and make the necessary changes to ourselves to promote behavior and experiences that we want. We're not changing to avoid triggering others but, instead, changing to promote peace in our spirit in the face of challenges. We're changing to be the best version of ourselves and move expeditiously toward our goals, whether they be relationship goals, financial, or spiritual. The only thing in the way of creating the lives we desire is us. We are the change we've been waiting for. If that's true then the next logical question is "What are we going to do to make the shift and bring about this change?"

When we did our processing work, we worked on solutions to resolving the triggers in STEP 4. We briefly discussed tools like LACING™, meditation, hypnotherapy, etc. as ways to challenge our conditionings and patterns. With Ownership, we go a step further and do two things: (a) make a final determination of that plan to resolve our traumas and (b) list out any other steps that we'll take to ensure that we'll hold ourselves accountable for moving forward into our newly desired behavior. Yes, it's true that we did some analysis in the Processing exercises in STEP 4 to figure out the tools that will work best for us, but, in reality, until you really own your stuff, we can't possibly expect to carry the work through until the end. The Processing work is beautiful work, but it's largely intellectual and still based, to a large part, in our Ego; therefore, its foundation is shaky until we commit to it and make ourselves accountable for the outcome. Thus, the Ownership step is to list out a specific plan of action as part of our Ownership Statement. The first part of the Ownership Statement was to do just that — take responsibility for our feelings and responses. The second part of the Ownership Statement demonstrates our accountability by listing an action plan.

Here's another example of what Ownership looks like when we add the action plan component. In this example, a coach who does online courses changes the terms with her students after selling the course to them because she felt it was offered too far below market value. This triggered the students to complain, which, in turn, triggered her. This is her ownership statement.

> Owner: "Ownership: I'm getting more clear. I own that decid-ing midstream that the class I taught will not have lifetime access like my other courses — not being clear about that, up front isn't optimal — for business or friendships. I own that I have not, in accordance conducted business with capitalist best practice for a great many years due to clashing concepts around friendship and business, which sets up wavering per-sonal integrity — like which am I really about here? It's been unclear, which casts lack of clarity into all my actions.
>
> "My plan of action (specific self-growth work) surrounds — #1: Strategize around what I desire to be here (business,

friendships, both, neither?) and how to clearly focus in that lane. #2: Lace fears around friendships, friendship patterns, mom's business/friendship quandary. #3: Place management of my relationship academy into the hands of managers who will decide how to handle said concerns. #4: Build personal integrity by truly being in my correct lane here — doing only what I'm told I'm best at and leaving all other functions to managers."

Notice in this ownership statement that her action plan includes both self-work to resolve the triggers as well as practical steps to change her business to be more efficient and run in integrity to increase client satisfaction. It's true the students were triggered by the change in policy for the class and it's true they were in their emotions about it, but it doesn't mean their concerns and observations weren't warranted. Once we come out of Ego and analyze our triggers, we can more objectively look at the feedback from others even when it's done out of anger and aggression.

Ownership Case Studies

Let's continue with our four case studies from the Venting and Processing sections and add the Ownership components.

Case Study #1: In this example, a husband is mad that his wife didn't tell him that she used to date one of his friends from college. He found out through another mutual friend at a party just last night and they've been married for twelve years.

> Wife: "Would you like to take ownership of your feelings from what you vented about the other day?"
>
> Husband: "Not at this time. I'm not quite ready."

Two weeks pass.

Husband: "I'd like to take ownership of the situation from a few weeks ago if you're willing to listen."

Wife: "Yes, I am."

Husband: "I'd like to take one-hundred percent ownership of the situation I created with you a few weeks ago. After further analysis and processing, I realized that I've always created these types of situations based on unresolved childhood traumas. Not only did I create the situation itself from my subconscious projection, but I also created the underlying feelings and emotions that accompanied the situation as well. Because of the childhood trauma and the emotions I felt during that trauma, I have an addiction to those same emotions and create situations where I can manifest them. So, yes, I realize this is all me. I create my life."

Wife: "You are heard. Do you have any strategies to resolve the story you're carrying from childhood."

Husband: "Yes, thanks for asking. My plan is to work with a new coach I hired to get to the root of that trauma and rewrite that story. They say it will take some work and dedication, but I'm ready for it. My goal is to gain my life back and let go of these petty jealousies."

Wife: "That's amazing. I love you."

The first observation is that the husband chose not to make his ownership statement at his wife's request. This is important because ownership is such a big step that you can only take ownership when you're absolutely ready to do it. No one can make you take ownership of anything, especially of an event that you were majorly triggered by. So was the wife wrong in asking the husband to take ownership? Absolutely not. It's her job to help facilitate the growth process and remind the husband that there's more work to do. Why? Because until the final gateway is completed — Gateway #4 — Gratitude, the situation is still open, just like a wound healing after an accident, and all parties are affected.

When someone is triggered due to something you've done or are a part of, you're also a part of that situation. You are immediately responsible for your part in the growth process, which may be to hold space and be the Witness as needed. In the case where you're not asked to be the Witness, you may still be a critical part of the process because your friend, wife, husband, or family has been triggered and is in pain, and you want to be supportive of their healing as someone who loves them and wants the best for them. Again, when we look at these situations as equivalent to open physical wounds, we see the criticalness of tending to them until their healed. The Ownership exercise is simply synonymous to putting hydrogen peroxide and a bandage on the wound, but until we've taken ownership, it's still exposed and in danger of infection.

End Ownership Exercise

Case Study #2: In this example, a wife suspects that her husband has cheated on her. The wife's friend sent her a picture of the husband out with another woman and being intimate with her (i.e., holding hands and kissing).

> Wife: "I'd like to take ownership of the cheating situation that came up for us last week. Are you willing to hear me at this time?"

> Husband: "Yes, I am."

> Wife: "I'd like to take ownership for creating the cheating situation. I realize now that I created that situation because it's what I expect to happen in my life. I expect to be disrespected, especially by the men in my life. This has come up for me numerous times before in different relationships and

with some work and friend scenarios as well. I believe this started for me from childhood and carried into my teenage years, but either way, I know I've created this, so I'd like to take ownership for the situation, my feelings of being disrespected, and how I reacted in the situation.

"I'd also like to communicate my plan to make some shifts in my life. I'm reading some books on releasing blame and guilt and seeking group support for living my best life. I really want to be more authentic in expressing who I am and not feel I need to hold others accountable for my happiness. So, it's a work in progress, but I'm on the path to growing in this area of my life.

"In terms of our marriage, I honestly can't say what I want to do at this point. I don't feel obligated to stay in the marriage just because, but I don't want to make any rash decisions either. I'd like to explore some resources in my personal journey before making any decisions about us, to be honest. I'd like you to know that my decision to leave or stay isn't centered around what happened with the cheating, but rather me reexamining what I really want for my life. That includes looking at why I entered this union to begin with, which I fear may include some of my insecurities rather than coming from a place of love for myself and you. If that's the case, it's not fair to be with someone who you didn't marry for love. I guess it's just a journey that I'm on right now, but please know that I don't blame you for what happened. I know you're doing the absolute best you can and that my feelings, emotions, and happiness are my responsibility, not yours. This is where I'm at right now, but I feel better already in taking full ownership of this situation and my life and not putting everything on you. It just feels like a major step forward for me."

Husband: "Thank you for sharing that and taking full ownership of the situation."

We need to make a few observations here. The wife did a great job in both taking ownership and laying out a plan of action. The most important thing she shared was reevaluating her life for her and not taking action based on the cheating events that caused her to be triggered in the first place. This is what Ownership is about. What's also important to observe here is that Ownership doesn't mean she's automatically going to stay in the marriage, but, instead, she realizes her part in the experience and claims power over it. However, we're all free to create our lives, and, in this case, creating her life may include choosing a new relationship path. It was smart of her to leave it open for further analysis and not make a snap decision or judgment on her marriage. Lastly, she began to acknowledge that her traumas may have been at the root of why she chose to be with her husband in the first place. This is a beautiful acknowledgment because these traumas usually affect our lives in a widely pervasive manner as opposed to just one isolated triggering episode or event.

Another important note is that the husband stayed in "Witness" mode and didn't react to his wife's statement about possibly leaving. In traditional, old paradigm relationships, her statement would have started an argument or made the other person defensive, but that's not the point. When the wife asked her husband to hold space for her as she claimed Ownership of the situation, he essentially agreed to be inside of his Higher Self as the Witness. This requires that he be out of his Ego and ignore his Animal impulses, which inevitably may have come up in the form of fight or flight because of his desire to save his marriage or save face in the light of public embarrassment from impending divorce.

End Ownership Exercise

Case Study #3: In this example, an employee has been passed up for promotion for the third time by someone they feel isn't as skilled or deserving as them. In this specific example, we're going to assume the employees at the company are trained in the UPLVL Communication™ protocols; thus, the employee is going to take ownership with their supervisor.

> Employee: "I'm ready to take ownership of me being triggered around being passed up for promotion this year. Are you willing to hear me at this time?"

> Supervisor: "I am."

> Employee: "I'd like to acknowledge my ownership of me being triggered for being passed up for promotion this year. I'd also like to fully own my feelings around it and my response to it. After I completed processing my vent, I realized this is a recurring theme in my life, but one that I've never addressed. I've never acknowledged that I'm the common denominator in all these situations where I seemingly get overlooked or passed by. Not only that, but in most of these situations, the feedback to me has been that I can do more or that I wasn't quite ready for the recognition. I've always stayed in victim mode rather than doing the self-work. So, it's obvious I'm creating this scenario in my life and I'd like to own it at this time.

> "My plan to resolve this is to actually listen to my supervisors and work hard to implement the feedback that's been given to me. I also plan to use my yearly evaluations as an action plan and allow my mentors and supervisors to hold me accountable to turning around the areas of improvement and making them strengths. The goal will be to not just accept average in these areas, but push them all to assets. Lastly, I feel there are some psychological components to this as well for

me, so I'd like to use my health benefits and get psychological support from a professional. I think some evaluation from a licensed professional who's seen this kind of thing in people can offer some assistance as well.

"So that's my ownership and plan of action. Do you feel I missed anything?"

Supervisor: "That's really great work. I would say you covered everything. The only thing I think you should consider is also allowing some peer reviews as part of your process as well. I think those who work side-by-side with you will have some valuable insights as well both professionally and socially that may support your efforts. But overall, I think you really nailed this and I'm looking forward to supporting you any way I can."

The primary observation here is that the employee asked for the supervisor's input for additional areas to take ownership or add to the action plan. This is a strong ownership indication because it proves that the employee is out of their Ego and open to guidance from others. This is important and represents a step into the Higher Self.

End Ownership Exercise

Case Study #4: In this example, a relationship coach is feeling that her friend is forcing free coaching sessions on her by coming to the house and discussing her relationship life. This friend has purchased coaching from her before in the past, but lately has seemingly been trying to get free coaching by leveraging her access via their friendship.

Coach: "If you don't mind, I'd like to take ownership of the conflict we had a few weeks ago. Are you open to hearing me?"

Friend: "Yes, I am."

Coach: "I'd like to own the situation I created with you when I felt super triggered by the fact that you were attempting to get free coaching from me as a perk of our friendship. I see exactly how I've created this situation in my life. I have a fear of not being valued for my services and I'm constantly creating and seeing where I don't feel valued. It's like I'm hypersensitive to it at this point. I also put myself into these scenarios by offering my services at a price that's lower than what I want, then feel bad about it later and take it out on friends, family, and good clients. I was so upset by what happened that it almost took me into a slight depression, but I know it's all me. These emotions are just supporting me in maintaining these false beliefs that say, 'I'm not worthy.' I'm over it. I accept that it's me and I'm making the change today to eliminate these types of feelings and scenarios from my life.

"My plan is to begin to charge the price that I feel good about and not change it for any reason. Even if I don't get any new clients or lose all my old ones, I'm not lowering my price. I'm taking a stand for me. I'll send an email to all existing clients and those who are following me and let them know of this change effective immediately. I'll continue to honor my existing pricing for those with whom I have contracts, but won't renew under those same terms. Integrity is more important than receiving money at any cost. I'd also like to do some work around my parents and maybe not feeling appreciated or something. I'm not really sure, but I want to make amends with them and take responsibility for my life. I don't want to hold anyone else accountable for my feelings or my life. It's really time at this point."

Friend: "You are heard. Thank you for sharing."

Not much to observe here beyond the coach taking solid ownership for her feelings and how she created the situation with her friend. She also had an action plan that addressed both the practical aspect of the trigger — the pricing for her services as well as the psychological aspect — her relationship with her parents. This is how we cover all the bases with ownership, as there are usually multiple areas to be addressed within our action plans. Sometimes, people only want to focus on the spiritual or psychological work but not do the practical work; but that's not balanced. Our outside world is a direct reflection of our thinking.

End Ownership Exercise

Gateway #4 — Gratitude

What is Gratitude

It's customary in our culture to be thankful for the good things and people in our life. When you receive a gift from someone, you say "Thank you." When you're helped and supported by friends and family, you say thank you and make a mental note to return the favor whenever you can. It's no different inside UPLVL Communication™ where we've done some amazing work with the support of those who've not only witnessed us and held space, but for those who were able to show us ourselves so clearly. Yes, if it weren't for the people who triggered us, we wouldn't have been able to get to the heart of our pain, trauma, and deep-seated conditionings. Isn't that a benefit? Doesn't that deserve a "Thank you"? I know it may be hard to conceive that we owe gratitude to those who've pissed us off, but we do because the purpose of life is growth and we can't grow without seeing where the growth needs to occur. We can't grow when we're stagnant with unaddressed traumas that are shaping our responses, behavior, and life. The truth is, if it were left to our intellectual mind to figure out where we needed to grow, we never would. We'd stay content, remaining in the safe zones of life and avoiding the pain. Yeah, we may go outside our comfort zone in certain places, but we'd end up avoiding most of the emotional pain points. Why? Because our Animal natures prefer comfort, safety, and pleasure. It's nothing personal. So, when we're offered the gift of sight, we should embrace it and be thankful for it.

I'm not saying to be thankful in the moment of the trigger, which is why Gratitude is Gateway #4. We're usually not in place to be grateful for painful experiences until after we've vented, processed, and taken full ownership because our Animal isn't about being grateful and our Egos can only get there after things make sense. Gratitude is really the voice of the Higher Self because it realizes that everything serves to further, as the I Ching would say. The Higher Self doesn't put a label on situations being good or bad but simply experiences our journey into expansion.

So, who exactly do we owe thanks too? We owe thanks to everyone involved in the situations who triggered us. Let's say we had a major argument and blowup during holiday dinner with the extended family. Maybe these types of gatherings are a point of tension every year. Then everyone involved are people we should be grateful for because they've all contributed to us being able to see ourselves better, and, without them, certain personal hang-ups would continue to go unseen. So let's be grateful to the entire family.

We'd also like to be grateful to those who've supported us in our Venting, Processing, and Ownership exercises. Those who were willing to hold space, offer support, soothe the Ego, ask open-ended questions, and most of all, for putting their Egos in check so that we may fully heal ourselves. This is amazing work and support because most people don't know how to check their own Egos on behalf of others, especially when they were involved in the triggering situation and may have their own triggers around what happened. We should be grateful for them.

There are two parts to showing Gratitude. The first is to simply be in a state of gratitude for the experience. You can say to yourself, "I'm so thankful and grateful that I've had the opportunity to fully see myself and grow to the next level of my development. This has been amazing." We can't overlook the power of personal acknowledgment of our situation. Just telling ourselves how we feel has a major impact on our perspective and how we feel. The second way to show Gratitude is to show it toward the people involved in the situation. It's literally telling people you're thankful and grateful for their support. For example, if someone helped you process your situation, you can say, "Thank you so much for supporting me in my processing work. That meant a lot to me. I'm grateful to you." That's it. Showing Gratitude acknowledges the effort each person put into being there for you and shows them you appreciate them. This will go a long way, especially if you need their support in the future because we can never know if something else might come up with some of the same people.

However, it's not recommended to show gratitude directly to those involved who haven't done their work or supported you or aren't aware of the work you've done. In other words, don't go up to the police officer who pissed you off for giving you a ticket and say you're thankful for their support because they won't understand the context you're coming from. You can let them know you appreciate them doing their job or that you have no hard feelings or that you're not upset with how things went down, but don't heap praise upon them for intervening in your life to uncover traumas. They'll just think you're crazy or have ulterior motives. Gratitude is only valuable when people are clear about why you're showing the Gratitude and when it's clear you're sincere about it.

There's another aspect of gratitude as well. We need to adopt the habit of celebrating anything we consider a victory in life. Overcoming a childhood trauma, acknowledging our Animal or Ego as the culprit in our feelings and actions, or resolving tenuous situations with the UPLVL Communication™ system is a victory if there ever was one. We need to not only acknowledge ourselves, but celebrate as well. The Gratitude can serve as that celebration and acknowledgment of victory over the Animal parts of us.

Just like our other gateways, we need to ask permission to offer Gratitude because we can't assume people are in a mental or emotional space to receive it. Gratitude is a gift. We're praising someone for their role in our lives and the efforts they've put forth in the UPLVL Communication™ process, so we'd like them to be ready to receive that praise. It should be noted, that many people have a hard time receiving praise and being at peace with it. In our culture, we believe in immediately offering praise back partly because we don't feel worthy and also partly because we fear standing out from our peer groups. We don't want to be put too high on a pedestal because it puts pressure on us to be great. This is the work of the person being the Witness during the Gratitude statement — to remain at peace and receive the offering of Gratitude without feeling the need to give it back.

Lastly, it's important that we express our Gratitude when we're really ready to do so. In most cases, after we've expressed Ownership, we're in good place to express Gratitude; however, those two gateways don't necessarily coincide together. We can truly be in a place of owning our reality, but not quite in a space of being completely grateful for that situation and all the people involved. We may need some time to get there, which is why Gratitude is its own gateway.

Gratitude Case Studies

Case Study #1: In this example, a husband is mad that his wife didn't tell him that she used to date one of his friends from college. He found out through another mutual friend at a party just last night and they've been married for twelve years.

> Husband: "Can I express my gratitude for you and everything that's happened between us regarding you dating one of my friends from college?"
>
> Wife: "Of course."
>
> Husband: "Thank you for holding space for me as I vented and processed through this. I know it's not easy to hear a vent without getting defensive or triggered, but you did just that. You were also supportive during my Processing exercise and that helped me get to the root of why I felt the way I did. So, again thank you.
>
> "I'd also like to say, I appreciate our marriage and the fact that it truly has been the source for much of my growth. I mean, this is just one example. Without us coming together, I may not have been able to see this part of myself and grow through it. All that to say, I'm grateful for our union."
>
> Wife: "You're welcome and I'm also grateful for you, our marriage, and this entire experience."

Short, sweet, and to the point. The wife shouldn't feel like she also needs to express any gratitude in this situation, but it's perfectly fine that she did. On another note, the husband expressed gratitude for both his wife's support and for their union because it's the combination of those two things that allowed this situation to come to a head. If they weren't married, the emotions would not have been intense enough for the husband to care who'd she been with in the past. In expressing gratitude for the marriage, the husband is acknowledging the Progressive Love™ tenet of the purpose is growth, which is critical to acknowledge out loud as a reminder for why they're together in the first place. Love doesn't come without growth.

End Gratitude Exercise

Case Study #2: In this example, a wife suspects that her husband has cheated on her. The wife's friend sent her a picture of the husband out with another woman and being intimate with her (i.e., holding hands and kissing).

Wife: "Can I share my gratitude with you?"

Husband: "Yes, you may."

Wife: "First, I'd like to say my love for you has grown over these past few weeks. To be honest, I feel like it's grown for myself as well. I've just seen so much that I hadn't seen within myself before. I was shocked to be honest because my entire life has been affected by some of my childhood traumas, and I had no awareness of this. I know this has been hard for both of us, and I want you to know I am thankful for you being with me throughout this entire ordeal. That means the world to me because things could have gotten ugly and we could have both done and said things that we may later regret, but, instead, we handled things in love and maturity, and I couldn't have done my part without you. So thank you for being there for me. It means the world to me."

Husband: "You're welcome."

This particular gratitude statement is even more impactful considering the wife isn't clear on what she's going to do with the marriage. She's not sure if she will leave or stay, but expressing her gratitude further shows she has a Higher Self perspective on everything that has taken place and really does appreciate this phase of her journey.

Also, the husband responded with a "You're welcome," which is all that's required. Again, we want to resist the temptation to say more or deflect the acknowledgment that's being given here. This is part of the work in the Gratitude exercise for the Witness. Can you receive a compliment and appreciation or do you feel the need to give a compliment back? There's nothing inherently wrong with complimenting someone back, but many of us do it because we don't know how to receive something and be at peace inside of that reception. We feel we need to do something in return, partly because we don't feel worthy of praise. As a Witness, our job is to stay inside of our Higher Self and observe the gratitude while remaining in a peaceful state. The Higher Self doesn't feel an impulse to do anything other than observe and experience. So, we can see the great amount of work that needs to be done on both sides.

End Gratitude Exercise

Case Study #3: In this example, someone has been passed up for promotion for the third time by someone they feel isn't as skilled or deserving as them. In this specific example, we're going to assume the employees at the company are trained in the UPLVL Communication™ protocols.

Note: The assumption here is that the Gratitude is being offered in the same meeting that the Ownership statement was given; thus, there's no need to seek permission to offer Gratitude.

> Employee: "I'd like to thank you for taking the time to work through this issue with me. It means a lot to my growth as a professional, but it helps my personal life too. From

my experience, most employers wouldn't work with their employees in this way, so thank you."

Supervisor: "You're welcome."

Notice how professional environments offer a different twist to the Venting, Processing, Ownership, and Gratitude exercises, yet they're still heartfelt and deep.

End Gratitude Exercise

Case Study #4: In this example, a relationship coach is feeling that her friend is forcing free coaching sessions on her by coming to the house and discussing her relationship life. This friend has purchased coaching from her before in the past, but lately has seemingly been trying to get free coaching by leveraging her access via their friendship.

Coach: "I'd like to offer some gratitude if you're available to hear it."

Friend: "I am."

Coach: "Thank you for supporting me through this process. I needed to move to a new level in my business consciousness and you were able to support me in that. This entire situation has also made our friendship closer because I believe these are the things we need to go through together to really be able to understand and support each other."

Friend: "You're welcome, and I agree this has made us closer."

End Gratitude Exercise

This concludes our case study examples.

"Communication leads to community, that is, to understanding, intimacy and mutual valuing."

~ Rollo May

Part 3 — The Pluralities

The UPLVL Communication™ toolset is so rich and intense. So many tools to support us in maximizing the effectiveness of our communications. The system also requires one to become accustomed to a new way of living. We realize the needed shifts in communication are all encompassing, but don't forget what we're doing here — we're literally attempting to rewrite how we speak to one another while compensating for inconsistencies in the English language itself. We're overcoming cultural norms that move us farther apart instead of bringing us closer together; to do this, it takes serious changes in how we speak and how we perceive one another. So, keep in mind, as we continue to introduce new tools and concepts, that the UPLVL Communication™ system takes practice. In addition, make sure to exercise patience with self as we learn this information and apply it. Over time and as we become more engaged in the system, things shift for the better in our relationships.

Up to this point, we've gone through an amazing set of communication exercises that are designed to bring us closer together in the midst of our challenges while also growing us in character. When utilized properly, UPLVL Communication™ leaves nothing to chance because it brings all communications into a container that allows order. That said, the truth is, most of our communications are organic in nature and take place outside of preset containers. Meaning, the Venting, Processing, Ownership, and Gratitude steps are intentional and require all parties to agree to participate.

What happens when the container can't be set or the people involved don't agree to be a part of our communications exercise? Well, we have chaos, which is basically the standard and accepted form of communication we see in Western relationships and in life in general. There's no judgment on chaotic communication for those who choose to participate in it because even though we have introduced the UPLVL Communication™ system, all of us will choose to participate in Ego-based communication at various points, partly because that's how we've been trained and also because the Animal and Ego aren't always going to give way for order. They just won't *feel* like it. The Ego and Animal sometimes want to express their views or emotions or have a desire to win. Again, no judgment. Welcome to the human experience.

Let's go back to our formula:

$$Life\ Creation = f(M, S, B)$$

So even in the midst of chaos, if we can align our minds, spirits, and bodies, we can create alignment, order, and peace regardless of what everyone else is experiencing. This brings us to The Pluralities.

Pluralities is an old English word meaning the fact or state of being plural. It comes from the Latin root meaning more than one. As we've previously determined, although we experience reality with others, we are actually, one-hundred percent, creating reality ourselves. In addition, we are, one-hundred percent, experiencing that reality by ourselves; because what we are experiencing is different than what others are experiencing.

The Pluralities in UPLVL Communication™ denotes five key language tools that we can easily access when needed. We use these tools when having discussions outside of the ordered and contained communications illustrated with the Venting, Processing, Ownership, and Gratitude exercises. In other words, the Pluralities are the tools to bring order in the midst of chaos. It's essentially our ability to insert the UPLVL Communication™ protocols into any situation we might find ourselves in; thus, allowing us to remain solution-oriented and maximize the opportunity to grow.

The good news is the Pluralities aren't entirely different from what we've already covered thus far, so picking them up shouldn't be too difficult. So, let's dive in.

There are five Pluralities. They are:

- Authenticity vs. Honesty
- Ownership vs. Apology
- Compassion vs. Compromise
- Perspective vs. Fact
- Open-Ended Discussion vs. Closed-Ended Discussion

Authenticity vs. Honesty

As a culture, we have essentially turned honesty into the divulgence of incriminating facts, which forces us into the act of considering whether we might like to be honest or not, based upon the how harshly we might be judged by the person receiving those facts. Because of judgment and the impending punishment following that judgment, we're rarely honest in this society. People might disagree with that, but even disagreement is part of our dishonesty. We'd like to believe we' re honest because it feels good to our Ego. What's the standard definition of honesty? To be free of deceit. That definition alone excommunicates pretty much all of us because being deceitful is also a culture thing. For example, the act of breaking the speed limit is an act of deceit because: (a) we only do it when we suspect we aren't being tracked and (b) we never go to a police officer after we've broken the speed limit and said, "Hi. I just wanted to be honest. I was about twenty miles over the speed limit for the past ten miles on the highway and wanted to be completely transparent with the authorities and face proper judgment."

Why does the government set up secret speed traps on the highway? Because they know we're often deceitful. They know if we realize we're being tracked we won't speed, so they need us to believe we're not being tracked. This is how the government can capture our honest driving behavior. Makes sense? Why do they set up secret red light and speeding cameras? Because they know if we see a couple of police officers working the intersection that it will change our driving behavior. Who gets caught by red light cameras the most? Those of us who don't live in the town and first offenders who didn't realize the camera was there.

In like manner, the government is being deceitful in setting up cameras to monitor behavior of drivers without informing the drivers of where the cameras are! So, both the government, set up to protect and serve, and the consumer or driver, are actually dishonest in the actions — both parties, both sides. Thus, is it factual that most of us are honest or lacking deceitful behavior? Let's utilize this simple example to conclude that no, we're not. And that doesn't infer bad behavior; it infers natural, human behavior.

Let's move to the dating world and assess our honesty. If we go on a first date, how often do we share our true thoughts of a person's habits, looks, or behavior? How often do we share our true intentions with them, for instance, "I really only want to have sex with you" or "I thought I liked you, but after being around you for five minutes, I'll just take the free meal and never call you again." or "This date was a bad idea." or "You're a nice guy, but your breath smells really bad." Is it becoming clearer now?

Think about how often we are simply not honest with those around us, especially in relationship situations. Again, we're not criticizing ourselves, but pointing out a cultural phenomenon that has a major impact on our ability to relate with one another. We hold so much back from one another because of fear of judgment, yet we expect our partners to divulge critical information to us when we want it.

How about during sex? Are we honest about how we're feeling, what we want, what we don't like, or if we really even want it in the moment? Are we honest with our partners about who we're attracted to, who we miss, who we'd like to have sex with, who we dreamed about, or what we really think of our sexual life together? Again, the answer is mostly "No" across the board and it's no slight against any of us as human beings, but just how we were conditioned to communicate and relate to one another.

One of the most stressful things we could imagine is our thoughts being downloaded into the minds of the people in our relationship and work lives. It's terrifying to even think about. Can you imagine being on a date and your thoughts suddenly being streamed onto their phone along with accompanying images? Yikes!

The point is, if we find ourselves not being honest in so many situations in life, is it really a fair expectation to hold others to that standard, especially when we can't do it ourselves? Is holding a partner to that standard of *being honest* a loving thing to do? Have we divulged all of our truths to them? We know the answer is "No" and we know why — because we're scared of judgment and punishment that will surely follow such divulgences. We understand the love between us is conditional. We understand that we don't truly accept one another for who we are, but rather the fantasy of who we want each other to be, and how a person can make us feel. It's not an incrimination; it's just the facts. It's best to just call it a wash and work toward another strategy — *authenticity.*

Authenticity is the act of: (a) knowing what voice is speaking and thinking in any particular moment and (b) communicating that voice along with whatever is being shared at that moment. We know the possible voices influencing our thoughts are the Animal, Ego, and Higher Self. It makes a huge difference because we all have an Animal, Ego, and Higher Self nature. We all know how these aspects of ourselves express things. Being Authentic simply means we will share a statement or utterance by first noting which of the energetics within us is speaking.

For example, if I'm on a date and I say, "My Animal (i.e., the bull) really wants to have sex with you badly right now. Like, it wants to clear the table and literally have wild sex in this restaurant in front of all these people. That's how sexy and beautiful you look right now." Sounds crazy to say that, right? That's what we call an authentic share because we identified the voice within us before we communicated and we also shared the identity of that voice during the communication. How about this communication, "My Ego feels like my mother won't like you because you have a lot of similarities to my ex-boyfriend and it has me kind of scared right now. I know it's just my Ego speaking, but it has me feeling like ending this date right now and blocking your number." If we're honest (pun intended), we can admit we have had similar thoughts before on dates.

So when do we use authentic communication? We use it all the time, but especially when someone is asking us to be honest. Remember, the advantage of the Pluralities is we can use these tools with anyone who doesn't know the UPLVL Communication™ system or when someone is speaking to us out of their Animal or Ego nature. We're attempting to bring order out of chaos or another way to say it is, we're attempting to inject the Higher Self in the midst of an Animal- and/or Ego-based conversation. Let's look at some examples.

Boyfriend: "Where were you last night? Were you at another man's house?!"

Girlfriend (using authenticity): "My Ego isn't wanting to share this information with you right now because it feels you're going to trip out no matter what I say. From a higher perspective, what you need to know is that all is well and I will share myself fully with you as I become able to do so. Right now my Animal is too frightened to share with you because it feels threatened. Plus, my Ego feels like it's none of your business where I was at last night, especially considering the fact that we're not married. It is just how my Ego is viewing the situation."

Boyfriend: "So you were at a dude's house last night. I mean, if you can't say no, then that must mean yes. So, yeah, you're a cheating *****."

Girlfriend: "This is an example of why my Animal doesn't want to communicate with you right now. It doesn't feel safe in your presence and as I stated before, my Ego really and truly doesn't feel like it's any of your business. My Ego's perspective hasn't changed in the past thirty seconds."

In this example, the boyfriend is fully in his Ego and Animal nature. He's angry and perhaps a bit scared that he's losing his girlfriend to another man; thus, it's difficult for him to be reasonable and rational about the situation. Let's say he doesn't know about the UPLVL Communication™ system and, therefore, doesn't know about setting container, but the girlfriend is familiar with the system. In this case, she understands that he's speaking from his Ego and Animal and immediately realizes that everything that he's saying is a lie; thus, there's no reason to take his words as truth or fact. This alone will help her stay centered in her Higher Self as much as possible and keep her away from being defensive in light of the accusations her boyfriend is making.

Because she identifies him as being in his Animal and Ego, she realizes that nothing she says can really be heard because her boyfriend is already triggered by the thought of her going to another man's house. So, she immediately invokes authentic communication instead of honesty, since honesty leads to incrimination and more triggers.

It's true that the boyfriend isn't going to like her authentic communication and even see it as avoidance or being passive aggressive, but, at least, the girlfriend is being authentic with him. At least, she's explaining how she feels and why she feels that way, and that will be respected in the long run.

It should be noted that she can also communicate to her boyfriend without using the words: *Animal, Ego,* and *Higher Self* so as not to confuse him, but it's a good practice to use these voice identifiers because it will help identify where she's coming from.

Setting Container

We can also set container when we want to speak authentically to our partner or anyone else for that matter. Let's say, the girlfriend is ready to have more authentic communication with her boyfriend regarding his accusation about her going to another man's house. She could set container before she speaks.

> Girlfriend: "May I speak authentically with you? I love you very much and I would like for you to know my actual thoughts on what's happening here."

> Boyfriend: "It's about time you said something other than that hocus pocus b*** s*** you've been talking."

> Girlfriend: "I was really in my Ego about you accusing me of going to another man's house, partly because we're not married but also because I already told you I was hanging out with my girlfriends. But now I'm in a place where I can speak to you from my Higher Self and not get offended or

aggressive with your accusations or the way you're coming at me. The fact of the matter is I went with Tasha to Club Verde until about 2am then came home. We did meet some guys there and they bought us drinks. We danced with them for most of the night, and I gave one of them my number. That essentially encapsulates the entirety of my night."

Boyfriend: "I don't even believe you, but at least you admitted you were out being fast when you're already in a relationship. Whatever. Keep your lie to yourself."

Girlfriend: "I understand you're still upset and don't believe me, but there's nothing I can do about how you feel. There are no words I can say that will put you in a place of happiness, so I'll just end the conversation here. The point is, you asked where I was and if I spent the night at a man's house, and I got to a place where I could answer you without being in my Ego, and I did."

The primary observation is that the girlfriend felt in control of herself enough to speak authentically to her boyfriend and answer his question honestly. She's not so deep in her Ego about the fact they aren't married, yet he's still acting like they are or that he owns her body or something. She was able to speak honestly about her entire night without regard of being judged or punished by her boyfriend. Why? Because she was able to connect with her Higher Self, which doesn't get into judgment or right or wrong and just be who she is authentically without the need to apologize or feel guilty or feel the need to appease her boyfriend's Ego. Until she was able to get to that point, there couldn't be a productive conversation about where she was, but only an Ego battle where the possibility of being triggered is increased.

Voice Identification

When we're having discussions with our partners, we should feel empowered enough to ask, "Who's speaking?" Meaning, we need to consistently send reminders to one another that we need to be mindful of where we are speaking from.

Ownership vs. Apology

Ownership is such a critical Plurality that it was assigned its own gateway — Gateway #3 — Ownership. So, we discussed this Plurality extensively already, but let's recap a few important points here because we'll be using Ownership outside of a container when applying these Pluralities.

There are a few good places to apply the Ownership Plurality:

1. in the midst of authentic communication as discussed in the Authenticity Plurality section and
2. when someone is demanding an apology from us.

Taking ownership during an Ego-based discussion is a great way to move the conversation toward the Higher Self and minimize the impact of the Ego's influence on the conversation. Generally, when speaking with someone who already believes we're wrong, bad, or inappropriate in our actions, we can recognize a learned desire they have for us to apologize. An apology, in Western culture, is an admission of guilt and way to elevate the Ego of one person over another.

This is the case because the Ego will jump at the chance to make itself look good by avoiding blame. There's no better way to look good and separate yourself from others than by making yourself the saint and others the villain. Taking ownership doesn't make us the villain, but to someone firmly in their Ego, it has the same effect.

Again, when taking ownership, be mindful to not take the blame for how the other person is feeling, but only how you created this situation that you're experiencing. This will require that you understand not only that you've created the scenario, but also that you understand the source for how this situation was created. Specifically, you understand why someone is in your face, firmly in their Ego, accusing you of violating them in some way. We could say, you've done some quick processing on the situation or that you've encountered something similar before and recognize what it is. For example, when my wife accuses me of not being a man and operating inside my feminine nature, I can understand how I created it because it's a recurring theme in our marriage, and I've had time to analyze and process it. So when it comes up again, I can immediately move to ownership as a way to dissipate the argument.

Wife: "Rakhem, you act like such a b**** sometimes, and it gets on my freaking nerves. I'm just tired of this!"

Rakhem *(ownership statement):* "I totally own that I've purposefully shied away from developing my leadership in business and finances over the years, so I know exactly why I've manifested this situation and specifically this criticism from you. I understand exactly why you're upset right now because my mom used to get upset at me the same way when I repeatedly lost my lunch money in school. I know that until I do the work to resolve those childhood emotions, you'll continue to see me in this way. This entire situation is my creation and I own that."

Wife: "I don't want to hear all that hocus pocus, airy fairy crap, Rakhem. Where's the money for the bills and groceries?!"

Rakhem *(authentic communication)*: "I understand how you feel and I empathize with you. I know it's hard to not have what you desire or feel you need. I don't have an answer right now, at least nothing you'd want to hear. I've already explained our current financial situation and what I plan to do to move us past this point."

Here we have ownership followed by authentic communication in the midst of a heated exchange. This is the best way to apply the Ownership Plurality outside of container.

Compassion vs. Compromise

What is compromise? It's doing something you don't want to do now in exchange for doing what you want to do later. We know that sounds normal to people because in our culture, we've been trained to not get what we want. We've been trained to not expect to do what we feel or want to do. It starts in childhood when you're told "No, No, No, No," to almost all your requests to the point where it becomes a subconscious pattern. We expect to be told no at almost every turn, which causes us to be antisocial and by ourselves so that we can at least do what we want. No roommate. No girlfriend. No boyfriend. No boss. No nothing. Just us, right?

What's the alternative? There's always the option of moving toward what you want and not compromising your desires for the sake of others feelings. Meaning, if I want to go out and my wife doesn't want me to go out, I can understand her feelings and emotions, but go out anyway. I can decide to be in a relationship that feeds me and when it doesn't, I can move on to one that does. I can honor what others want to do and allow them to do it even if I'm in my feelings about it, so that I can afford myself the same freedoms. We're much more empowered as human beings when we offer others the same freedoms we desire for ourselves. It's called acceptance and unconditional love. You do you and I'll do me and when we're in alignment, we'll do us together. However, just because we did us yesterday, doesn't mean we'll do us tomorrow. We'll have to see.

The truth is that compromise leads to resentment. If I'm doing something I really don't want to do, but I do it anyway, I've just brought anxiety and stress into my body, especially if this type of compromise becomes a habit. This is what makes people resent their partner and marriage — all the things they feel they have to do but don't want to do. Is that what marriage is? Spending thirty-three percent of your time doing things you don't want to do, another thirty-three percent doing what you want to do, and the final thirty-three percent living in neutrality. Pretty accurate formula, huh? That's a sad life, though, and we know it's the standard for many of us: spending our lives working a job we hate because it pays the bills and living with someone we've lost passion for while our health and happiness deteriorates. We try to compensate for it with intoxicants like alcohol, drugs, television shows, gambling, social media addiction, and the like. That's what compromise has gotten us; meanwhile, those who don't compromise go on to have wild success in life and refuse to take a back seat to anyone or anything that takes away from their happiness.

When has fifty percent ever been a good score? We'll do what you want fifty percent of the time and what I want fifty percent of the time. Take a moment to think about all the areas of your life where you've compromised. How did it feel? Authentic? Freeing? Empowering?

Here's a secret — you don't have to compromise in life. You don't have to compromise inside your relationships. It's possible to have a thriving relationship without compromise. How? Compassion.

Compassion is the act of embracing and acknowledging how others feel when there's a conflict of interests or desires. We're acknowledging them in the same way we're acknowledging ourselves. It's understanding they probably feel just as strongly about what they want to do as we do about what we want to do, so we totally get it. It's one-hundred percent real for them and nothing to be dismissive of. From that space, we can work through any disagreement on desires and activities.

Caveat: Are we advocating to never compromise or that compromise is bad? No, we aren't. Compromise isn't a bad thing. It only becomes a destroyer of relationships when it's the standard for negotiating differences of desire. It's only destructive when we're not mindful of what compromise is and does to ourselves and our partners and, thus, the relationship as a whole. That said, let's look at the difference between mindless compromise versus mindful compromise.

Mindless Compromise: "Okay, I'll stay home with you all this week. After all, I did go out all last week. I'm here. Let's have some fun."

So, all week, they'll do what they don't want to do. How do you think that will actually go over? How often will it enter the person's mind that they'd rather be doing something else instead? How often will they hold their partner accountable for the inevitable sadness or anger they'll feel as a result of this compromise? We all know the answers because we've all been there.

Now let's look at mindful compromise, which is the only compromise you should do.

Mindful Compromise: "Okay, I'll stay home with you all week. After all, I did go out all week last week. I'm here, but I'm doing this because I want to increase my ability to enjoy myself wherever I am. Thank you for this opportunity. I want this growth."

Here we have a different scenario. We have someone acknowledging their authentic feelings about the situation and taking on the challenge of growing in the process. This is what we mean when we say, relationships are for the purpose of growth because in order to make it work, you must grow yourself beyond where you currently are. You must decide to take on challenges. In this case, this is conscious compromise in which the person says, "This is a great opportunity to get beyond some of my innate tendencies and behavioral conditionings. Let me do this for me so that I can be better."

It's important to only take on these personal growth challenges when you want to and not at the behest of your partner, or else resentment again will set in. But what if we don't want to take on the personal challenge of growing beyond our comfort zones? How do we handle the request to stay home all week? We move to compassion.

Compassion: "Okay, listen. I know I was out last week, but I feel I'd like to go out this week too. I know that might hurt your Ego and make your Ego pretty upset. I'm willing to call you this week and check on you, but if I stay home with you instead of going out, I'll begin to resent you, and we won't have much of a relationship either way. Can you understand that? I love you and I have so much compassion for you. Before I go, let's think of things you can do while I'm gone. I'd love to support you with that!"

In this case, the person isn't going to do what they don't want to do, and they explain why. In addition, they offer compassion for how the other person is feeling and fully acknowledge the authenticity of their request. They even offer other ways they'd love to support them in lieu of the fact that they won't be there this week. Is this a form of compromise to support them so they can feel better while they're gone? No, it's just them wanting to support them because that's what their love for them would naturally lead them to do anyway. Just because someone chooses to do what they desire, doesn't mean they don't love the person. It simply means, they're choosing their self first while also supporting the other person in the best way they can.

As with our other Pluralities, we can set container and offer compassion to our partners or others.

> Wife: "Would you allow me, for a moment, to offer some compassion to you?"

> Husband: "Yes."

> Wife: "I'm speaking from my Higher Self here and with profound love for you. I realize you'd like me to stay home this week; however, I'm authentically not there yet. But I love you and would love for you to see this as a growth area for us."

This can also work in reverse where the other person requests compassion from their partner.

> Husband: "I realize you don't want to stay home with me this week because it's not in alignment with what you're authentically feeling. However, do you feel that you could offer me some compassion at this time because I really wanted you to stay with me?"

> Wife: "Yes, I can offer you compassion. I'm speaking from my Higher Self here and desire for us to continue to grow in love together. I understand that you want me to stay with you this week and I know that's an authentic feeling and desire for you. I honor that and appreciate that you want me to be here with you. I love you deeply and only want the best for you and us. I would love to stay with you, but I'm choosing not to only

because I want to stay in alignment with my authentic self. I want to honor myself and not feel resentful toward you or this relationship. Additionally, I'd like to support you in any way I can to finding things you can do and focus on while I'm gone. I'll also reach out to you consistently to check on you as well."

Husband: "That feels better. Thank you."

We should notice that there are elements of authentic communication throughout these compassion statements. People are speaking their truth as the reasons for their actions. There's also an element of ownership as well where people are owning how they feel as their feelings.

Perspective vs. Fact

We've talked a bit about what we perceive and how we perceive it. The main question is — Is what you're perceiving and sensing an accurate view of that reality? Or asked another way, is your perception of a particular reality in line with the perception of others? If not, by what percentage are those perspectives different? Ten percent? Twenty-five percent? Fifty percent? These are the questions we need to answer, but as we've illustrated in Part 1 of this book, our perspectives are largely colored by our personal story around the reality we're perceiving. For example, we could send two people into a low-income neighborhood in the middle of the city and one person sees poverty and despair and the other person sees a goldmine waiting to be exploited. Two teachers look at a troubled student and one teacher sees a child who is lost and probably headed to prison while the other teacher sees an artistic and creative genius who needs the proper guidance and stimulation.

In those examples, is one person right while the other person is wrong or are they both simply perceiving based on their story?

So let's break down perspective. A perspective is someone's Ego-based and personalized, stylized, and filtered story about what happened in a particular scenario. Perspective cannot be changed as it's a fixed reality and tied directly into the story related to that reality.

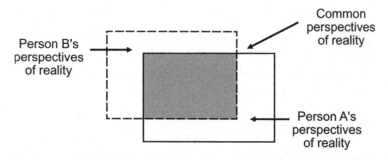

So then what's a fact? A fact is common perspective of something that aligns with a majority of other people's perspectives. We'll find that facts vary from time to time and from culture to culture. In other words, facts are subject to the variables of time and space — who's perceiving the reality, from what culture are they a member, and from what story are they comparing it too. It's a bit difficult to believe that facts are subject to time and space variables, but it's true. Just like at one time, there were cultures who believed the Earth was flat and other cultures that believed the Earth was elliptical. In both cases, neither culture could be convinced otherwise. In some cultures and religious organizations, the existence of God is a fact, while in others, it's not. We're not here to argue what is and isn't fact, but simply to explain what facts are and how we should leverage them in our communications. People tend to get very defensive about the facts they believe in, thus, making conversation about those facts impossible. For example, we can't talk to a religious person about the existence or quality of God without a level of defensiveness. In the same way, we can't talk to a scientist about the quality or existence of gravity, the speed of light, or the quality of bacteria. Is it because people don't want to grow and learn something new? No, it's not usually that, but instead, the culture we live in. People today make their living based on facts, and questioning those facts could destabilize what they've built and established over decades of their life as well as adversely impact their money. These things are more complex than meets the eye, as we're psychologically connected to facts and perspectives in ways that are difficult for us to know or accept. The fact (pun intended) of the matter is, our Egos tend to be heavily invested in certain facts and realities, and as long as that's the case, healthy communication is impossible.

Where does this leave us? Well, in summary, facts are weak when it comes to relationships. That's just a fact (smile). Most of the arguments, disagreements, and miscommunications come from people declaring their perspectives (i.e., beliefs) as facts and being super emotionally invested in those perspectives to the point where we attempt to force our partners to accept our perspectives as fact when they're not. Let's look at an example.

Sharing of facts: "You came home at 9pm. I texted you. See, it's right here! You also have come home late every day by thirty minutes. What are you up to?"

The facts-based conversation is accusatory and closed. It doesn't allow for another perspective, but instead looks to indict the person. There's no love or understanding in a facts-based conversation. There's no ownership or acknowledgment that one's perspective might be specific to that person only. In short, a facts-based conversation only leads to defensiveness, feelings of guilt and shame, a desire to escape the conversation, and feelings of anger and resentment toward the person instigating the conversation. Again, although we can agree on perspectives and, thus, call some of these perspectives facts, the reality is they aren't true and painting them as true is divisive and even violent.

The other danger with the facts-based conversations is that it empowers the Ego and Animal aspects of ourselves to control and steer the communication, which almost always guarantees it won't be effective. When we have access to a fact, it's human nature to get emotionally charged behind that fact and even be aggressive toward others to defend it. In the above example, is the point that the person came home late or is it that someone may be feeling fearful of the health of the relationship because they're seeing behavior they haven't encountered before? Is the point that the person is coming home late or is it that one of partners doesn't feel close enough to the other to communicate some important feelings they're experiencing that might be causing them to change their behavior?

Sharing of Perspectives: "It's my understanding that you're coming home late. That's just my perspective though. I'd love to hear yours. Mine is based on lots of things. My mom for instance used to get upset at my dad each time he came home late. So I have pattern stuff shaping my perspective. What's yours?"

When we share perspectives, we do a few things: (1) we take ownership of our feelings and perspectives and (2) we communicate authentically with one another. This opens everyone up to hearing what's being said without defenses going up because the person is taking responsibility from the very beginning of the conversation. This is what's most important in relationships — that we are open, receptive, and kind to one another. Relationships are not about proving the other person wrong or forcing someone to accept your reality or beliefs because that would be abuse actually. Relationships are about loving one another and working together, especially once you've made the choice to commit to someone. What is really that urgent where life hangs in the balance if your perspectives aren't accepted as facts? Nothing really. If you're with someone and things are that contentious and there's zero trust, openness, compassion, and love, then maybe you need to rethink that relationship anyway. Just a thought.

Open-Ended Discussion vs. Closed-Ended Discussion

We always have to go the foundation of why these communications protocols are useful. Currently, in relationships, people's Egos speak to one another. What is the Ego's goal? To separate itself as special and acquire public credit for its accomplishments and uniqueness. The Ego isn't bad. It's just here to do what it does. So, if the Ego wants to be right and we're primarily using our Ego to speak to one another, then what's the probable outcome of those discussions? Positioning, credit seeking, and wanting to look good in front of others, instead of solutions that serve the greater good. But what about the many problems that have been solved and conflicts that have been successfully resolved by people's Egos? Maybe it was Higher Self at work. Maybe the solution was found because someone's Ego wanted credit for finding a solution. Again, the Ego isn't bad, but it does have self-interests.

That leads us to discussions, debates, arguments, and why many of them are ineffective. The truth is, coming together in happiness isn't something that's fulfilling to most people's Egos unless someone receives credit for the resolution or coming together. So, we must figure out a way to take Ego out of the conversation.

Everything we've talked about thus far is a great help for that — authentic communication, ownership, speaking to one another with compassion, and having the right perspective are important foundations for eliminating the Animal and Egoic influences in our daily communications. Another final element is having Open-Ended Discussions (OED) instead of Closed-Ended Discussions (CED).

A CED is essentially an interrogation of the persons we're speaking to. CEDs have a goal of establishing proof of wrongdoing, admission of guilt, finding out what is wrong with someone, etc. These types of discussions cause people's defenses to go up. They dig in and attempt to say things that will make them look good or, in some way, discredit the accuser. Very rarely will someone want to take ownership or speak with compassion when they're in the middle of a CED because the adrenaline and cortisol levels are too high to be inside of the Higher Self. The result is endless conflict, hurt feelings, shame, guilt, and resentment for those who we perceive to be on the attack. Let's look at an example of a CED.

Closed Ended Discussion Example:

Person 1: "You're way past your prime."

Person 2: "So you're saying that I'm old?! What exactly did you mean when you said, 'I'm past my prime'? I think you need to explain yourself because you've made these kinds of slick comments before and I just let it go, but I'm calling you out today. Enough is enough! You better start talking right now or this might get real ugly quick. Today is your last day disrespecting me."

Does this statement fill our hearts full of love and compassion or put us on the defensive? If we're authentic with ourselves, we can even feel our cortisol and stress levels rise a bit just from reading a statement like this. Why? Because we've all experienced something similar before and it didn't have anything to do with love, understanding, or compassion. It didn't have anything to do with resolving conflict, but rather casting blame on someone and invoking feelings of shame within that person with the goal being humiliation and eventually an apology. These types of statements don't lead to any place good.

When Person 2 said, "You're saying I'm old?!" we see their Ego is taking what Person 1 said to them as fact as opposed to perspective. Person 1's statement of them being past their prime is simply an Ego-based perspective. It has absolutely zero bearing in reality, unless we all decide to make it so. But let's assume that Person 2 is unable to separate Person 1's perspective from fact. Instead, they can use OED as a way to gain clarity and understanding of what Person 1 is referring to before drawing any conclusions. Here's an example of an OED.

Open Ended Discussion Example:

> Person 2: "I've noticed that your perspective seems to be that I'm old or past my prime in some way, but I'd like to fully understand your perspective so that my Ego doesn't take things the wrong way. Plus, I feel my inner Animal nature getting a bit scared and defensive, so I'd rather have an open-ended discussion about it. Are you okay with that?"

> Person 1: "Sure. Whatever."

> Person 2: "Do you feel that I'm too old to be effective at my craft?"

> Person 1: "Honestly, I think you've lost a step or two. Things aren't getting done like they should. That's what I'm seeing, and I'm not the only one seeing that. It is what it is."

> Person 2: "Thank you for answering. May I ask you another question?"

Person 1: "Go for it."

Person 2: "Do you feel my inefficient performance can be corrected or do you believe that there's nothing I can really do because it's really just an inevitability of my age?"

Person 1: "To keep it all the way real, I think you can fix it, but you're operating based on your past accomplishments. Like, most of the staff here doesn't know what you did twenty years ago or any of that. Maybe the old school workers do, but not the younger folks. They can only judge based on what they're currently seeing, which, in my opinion, is an average level of effectiveness. Maybe if you just worked with the rest of us like a team instead of like you have tenure, we would see you differently, but trust and believe, you're not better than any one of us."

Person 2: "Thanks again for sharing that. I feel like I'm more aware of what you're saying. Do you have any questions for me?"

Person 1: "Nah."

There's usually a deeper truth underneath people's comments and criticisms of us, but if we're unable to have a conversation with an open mind and heart then we won't be able to get to those deeper understandings. In this example, we discovered that the primary complaint wasn't even rooted in age, but in a lack of connection to the rest of the work staff. It was more of an air of superiority that was being criticized. Or another way to look at it — Person 2's air of superiority was triggering to Person 1's Ego to the point where they had to say something about it to release the tension around that trigger. Person 1 may have even felt scared or threatened by Person 2's tenure at the workplace, which could have put their inner Animal nature into fight or flight mode, leading to the conflict.

What separates OED from CED is that there is no retort or response to a person's statement because that leads to further stress and defensiveness. We literally close the door to resolving the conflicts when we respond because of the natural adrenal rush that comes from our Animal nature. This is especially true when we're in our Egos.

Another way to look at a CED is through what's called an endless loop in the computer-programming world. It's when energy, in the form of code instructions, continues in a circular fashion forever and never escapes that circle. That's why it's called an endless loop. Think of OEDs as error processing where we're catching Ego statements and putting them into an error protocol so they can be properly processed, thus, keeping the overall program operational and running smoothly. Think of it as avoiding catastrophe. This is partly accomplished by asking permission to speak (i.e., setting container) each time a question is asked or an authentic statement is made. For example, "May I ask you another question?" Or, "Can I make an authentic statement about what I'm observing regarding your assessment of my work performance?" Additionally, during an OED, we ensure that we allow others to speak until their done and never cut them off mid-sentence. This is a critical aspect of having an effective OED and where we see many CED fall off the rails. The truth is, people aren't usually interested in really listening to what's being communicated by the other person. They're really only interested in pushing their perspectives as facts and the person they're talking to can usually feel this. Lastly, when having an OED, it's critical that we focus on actually listening to what's being said. This takes energy, focus, and discipline, but it's what separates OEDs from CEDs. This is much different than a CED where no permission is asked to speak (i.e., fertile soil for rudeness and defensiveness), people often cut each other off mid-sentence, and no one is actually listening to each other. No one is attempting to understand where the other person is coming from or how they're feeling.

In the above example, we saw a series of opened-ended questions used as the foundation for the OED, but more communication tools can be applied. The OED essentially brings everything together in an organic way, enabling us to have full conversations while keeping our inner Ego and Animal at bay.

OED can include:

- Venting
- Processing
- Ownership
- Gratitude
- Open-Ended Questions
- Authentic Sharing
- Compassion
- Perspective Sharing

OED can also include unsolicited:

- Empathy
- Reassurance
- Touch
- Simulation

Literally, entire conversations can be had with thoughtfulness and civility, leading to sanity in our relationships. Again, the primary rule of OEDs still applies — no retort. We are simply allowing ourselves the space to express in ways that bring clarity to what could otherwise be a tenuous situation.

Here's an example of bringing all the elements together in OED.

Case Study #5: A husband has found out that his wife has a child he didn't know about back home in St. Croix. She had the child at age eighteen then moved to the United States at age twenty-one. He met her when she was twenty-four and they married two years later. At this point, ten years later, they have two children and a house in a metropolitan area. The husband found out about his wife's other child at a family event when some of her extended family attended and talked about it in his presence.

At this point, the husband and wife have already gone through the venting and processing exercises, but the husband experienced a resurgence of feelings and emotions after watching a movie where a love child was discovered. The following is a conversation between them using the Pluralities.

Husband: "Can I ask you an open-ended question?"

Wife: "Yeah, sure."

Husband: "No one is wrong here. I'm just asking questions to appease my Ego. Can you tell me again why you thought it was alright for you to not tell me you had a daughter back home in St. Croix? I mean, I know we've been through this before, but I guess I'm still confused."

Wife: "To be honest, like I told you before, I was super scared of being judged, so I wasn't able to be authentic. My inner Animal felt threatened at the thought of men here in America knowing I had a child already. It ended up, my Animal never felt comfortable with it and my Ego created a justification to hide it for life basically. Plus, my Ego never really believed you would find out about it."

Husband: "Thank you for sharing."

Wife: "You're welcome."

Husband: "I need to vent right now. Are you willing to hear me out?"

Wife: "Yes."

Husband: "Thanks. No one is wrong. I realize I create my life and no one is doing anything to me. I realize my triggers are a result of stories I've accepted over the course of my life and those stories are shaping my perceptions in real time.

"It's still just a f*cked up feeling to be honest. Now my Ego is feeling all this pressure to bring your daughter up here to live with us even though you left her down there in the first place. I feel like I'm going to take a major hit to my name as a man and as a father with a step-daughter out there living in a third-world country. It's just totally f*cked up. It's a major development when I wasn't even expecting it, and it could have been avoided with some honesty in the beginning. I'm just confused and pissed right now and I still resent you for not telling me. It makes me wonder what else you're hiding from me or if you are even capable of being honest with me. Are you faking orgasms? Do you even like or love me? Did you marry me for my money or for status? Or maybe this was all a part of the plan to not tell me initially, but have me find out later then guilt me into bringing her up here. Maybe that was the plan when you decided to leave her there in St. Croix. I thought I was mostly over this, but I'm not because it's still an issue in my face. I'm totally not comfortable with this; not at all. That's it."

Wife: "How can I support you?"

Husband: "I guess I just need a hug and back rub."

Wife: *Hugs and holds her husband.*

Husband: "Thank you."

Wife: "You're welcome."

Husband: "I'd like to offer you some empathy if you're open to hearing it."

Wife: "Sure."

Husband: "I know that must have been hard because the truth is most men would judge you based on the fact you have a child back home. To be honest, I wouldn't have married you more than likely, and I can't say that I wouldn't have done the same thing as you if I had a child in another country. I totally understand how your inner Animal was scared about revealing the truth. I've been in a similar situation before in a past relationship. I had just started dating a young lady when I got a call from my ex-girlfriend that she was pregnant. Her and I had sex about a week before I met my new girlfriend. Anyway, I got really scared and decided not to tell my new girlfriend because I didn't want to lose her. My ex-girlfriend ended up having the baby, but the DNA tests showed I wasn't the father. The point is, I never told her about that entire ordeal, so trust me when I say that I know exactly how you were feeling."

Wife: "Thank you. That felt good to my Ego. Can I share something authentically with you?"

Husband: "Sure."

Wife: "After we had been together for a while, I really fell in love with you. I wanted to tell you about my daughter because I've never felt so safe with a man before in my entire life. My Animal felt totally safe and secure with you, but my Ego didn't see a reason why I should share. It felt the only possible outcome would be an end to the relationship. All that said, I'm grateful to you for being in my life and supporting us through this process of improving our communications. You've shown up for me in ways I can't even describe. Thank you."

Husband: "Thanks for sharing that and you're welcome. Before we end this conversation, I'd like to take ownership of this situation."

Wife: "Go ahead."

Husband: "I totally own how I created this entire situation including my current feelings around it. I realize my value system in looking for a wife was about superficiality and not substance. I realize my Animal partly wanted a trophy who could make me feel more like a man, and, in doing so, it didn't create space for you or any woman to totally trust me where they could open up with their deepest, darkest secrets. I get what you're saying about you feeling safer with me than any other man, but there was still more work for me to do. I didn't want to hear about some aspects of your life, truth be told. I didn't really ask enough questions. I never wanted to go to your home town and visit or meet your extended family. That's all on me. So, I take complete ownership here. I get it."

Wife: "Thank you. You are heard. I'd also like to take ownership of this situation and offer some empathy as well."

Husband: "Sure, go ahead."

Wife: "I can totally see how I created this entire situation for myself. My mistrust of men comes from my upbringing back home, but I've never really felt betrayed by men. I've never really seen a solid reason not to share my life or my truth with the men in my life. I just adopted the stories given to me by many of the women in my family without really questioning it, and that kind of messed me up. So when I did have the chance or feeling of wanting to share, I never really could. Not even with you, the man I loved the most. So, of course, I created a situation where my husband wouldn't trust me and where that lack of trust would be justified. This was totally avoidable. I know you said that you probably wouldn't have married me if you knew I had a daughter back home, but I don't believe that's necessarily true. I believe that you would have still married me, and, if not you, then someone still would have because they loved and accepted me for me. The more I run from myself, the quicker I find myself. So, I own this situation.

"Lastly, I'd like to let you know I honor how your Ego is feeling in this entire situation. My Ego would feel totally betrayed if this had been done to me, so I'd like to offer you some serious empathy right now. You've been through a lot with this situation and that shouldn't go unnoticed."

Husband: "Thank you."

End of Case Study #5 Example

There's so much to say about the exchange between this couple, but let's start with the fact that they are both bought into the UPLVL Communication™ system and are comfortable enough using it. The only way they get to this place is by practicing and using the system in real life and seeing the benefits. The overall assumption is that they both see the benefits in using the system. Next we can look at the fact that the Husband asked permission to ask a question knowing they were coming from a place of emotion. This sets the tone for the entire conversation going forward. That said, it's suggested that each person remind each other to set container when possible. The truth is, when we're feeling emotional our Animal deeply desires to express itself, and, in doing so, setting container is often the last thing that we think about. In that instance, the other person should remind them to set container before allowing them to vent or ask questions.

In this example, the Husband was already triggered before he asked the open-ended question, but got even more triggered afterward and moved to venting. This was the right thing for him to do because he obviously needed an outlet for that emotion he was feeling.

The most important observation is that the Wife also took the liberty to express herself as well. She decided to share authentically, take ownership, and offer empathy to her Husband. This exchange solidifies the "discussion" part of the OED, meaning, the ability to go back and forth inside of container with a level of sanity. This is critical because we want people to feel like this process can flow without being overly formal; thus, the introduction of the Pluralities.

Conclusion — Hope for a Sane World

"Many can argue — not many converse."

> ~ A. Bronson Alcott

EVERY ARGUMENT IN THE history of mankind is essentially about who's right and who's wrong. UPLVL Communication™ is the end to all arguments because its very basis is four key principles called The Progressive Love™ Tenets:

- No Shame, No Blame
- No Victims, No Villains
- No Cop Outs, No Drop Outs
- The Purpose is Growth, The Benefit is Love

The verb or action step present in these principles is clear: *I create my life.*

These principles create a solid basis to construct a system of language that aligns succinctly to them.

There is no more need to utilize the language as a language of war. Once we understand how to utilize this vast system that completely reformulates how we think, and what we believe — actually — we can begin to have communications with others rather than arguments.

UPLVL Communication™ completely obliterates who is wrong and who is right. The system opens our eyes to the field outside of right and wrong. That field is one of harmony and peace. We're not speaking metaphorically; there's literally a field or space of consciousness where humans can realize true attunement.

The four steps of UPLVL communication — Vent, Process, Ownership, and Gratitude — take us through a winding path to peace.

ABOUT THE AUTHORS

KENYA K. STEVENS, founder and CEO of JujuMama, considers herself a Love Shaman. She is a relationships expert, love coach, best-selling author, wife, and mother of three. Kenya attended Howard University in Washington D.C. where she graduated in 1997 with a degree in Education/Child Psychology. Not only did she scoop up a degree but she also met and married a fellow Howard graduate student Carl E. Stevens, Jr. Carl and Kenya have been married for over twenty-four years and now live in the mountains of North Carolina.

CARL E. STEVENS, JR., also known as Rakhem Seku, is a relationship expert, life coach, and best-selling author, husband, and father of three – and cofounder with Kenya of the Progressive Love Academy (PLA) — an online relationships and empowerment school designed to support people in creating the life, love, and marriages they desire. Carl has two degrees, one from North Carolina State University (NCSU) in Industrial Engineering and one from Howard University, an MBA with a finance concentration.

Beyond their college degrees, Kenya and Carl have been formally trained in yoga, breathing, meditation, and metaphysical thought for over ten years. They used these disciplines to formulate their unique coaching style. In 2005, Carl and Kenya cofounded JujuMama. Using the skills and unique empowerment tools they refined for years, the Progressive Love™ Movement and Progressive Love™ Academy (PLA) was formulated in 2007 after broad success in coaching couples and saving marriages since JujuMama's inception.

The Stevens reach individuals deeply, supporting them in creating harmonious relationships, and achieving life desires. Utilizing JujuMama's success, Kenya and her husband Carl have expanded the Progressive Love™ Academy into a powerful resource for coaches and couples! They have created the first relationship academy that provides a platform for their certified coaches to teach. Over 250 love coaches, tantra practitioners, and manifestation coaches have been certified through PLA. With a flailing 55% divorce rate, the pair is sure we need new alternatives. Carl and Kenya believe Progressive Love can save the modern relationship.

One alternative style that the Stevens believe is aiding couples in becoming more authentic is Freedom Based Relating or Polyamory. The couple has curated a vast library of content covering topics such as love, sex, relationships, tantric sex, metaphysics, astrology, and more. The Stevens have been featured in *EBONY* Magazine (February 2010 & November 2011), The Mo'Nique Show™, The Michael Baisden Show™, Fox News, Dr. Phil Show™, Rikki Lake Show™, The Brian Cunningham Show™, and over 300 Talk Radio and blog shows.

Carl E. Stevens, Jr. (aka Rakhem Seku) is also a metaphysician and teaches the Bagua Astrology System (BAS) and applies metaphysical concepts to support people in creating the lives they desire through the Progressive Love™ Academy (PLA)

Carl is the author of numerous books, including:

- *The Art of Open Relating: Volume 1 - Theory, Philosophy, & Foundation*
- *Tame Your Woman: Become the Man She Needs*
- *Manifesting Marriage for Women: 9 Steps to Finding Your Partner and Creating a Successful Marriage*
- *I Create My Life: Manifesting Your Desires Using the Sun Cycle*
- *Bagua Astrology Oracle Interpretation Guide*
- *Bagua Astrology Character Mapping Interpretation Guide*
- *Bagua Character Map: Science, Analysis, & Interpretation*

- *Moon Manifestation System Workbook & Journal*
- *Bagua Astrology for Beginners*

Kenya is the author of:

Change Your Man: Become the Women He Desires
Memoir of an Opening Marriage (coming soon)

At the Progressive Love Academy (PLA), students are certified in the many disciplines Carl and Kenya have created and authored including:

- UPLVL Communication™ Certification
- Life & Love Coaching Certification
- Feminine Power Certification
- i2Tantra Certification
- Moon Manifestation System Certification
- Bagua Astrology System (BAS) Certification
- Three Way Mirror Certification

Carl and Kenya have hundreds of audios and videos available to their students at the Progressive Love™ Academy and additional products available to the general public through their store.

To contact Kenya and Carl, you can email them at mail@jujumama.com.

You can find their Facebook fan page at http://www.facebook.com/progressiveloveacademy

The website for the Progressive Love™ Academy is located at http://progressiveloveacademy.com

The Progressive Love Academy (PLA) is your #1 relationship tools and information resource online school on the web for creating your life and ideal relationship. No other online relationship school has the amount of tools, resources, and certification courses.

With courses and certifications like:

- UPLVL Communication™ Certification
- The Relationship Tools Video Library
- The Trust Forum
- The Three Way Mirror Certification Course
- Feminine Power 101
- The Blue Butterfly Women's Initiation
- The Peaceful Warrior Men's Initiation

For more information go to:

https://www.progressiveloveacademy.com

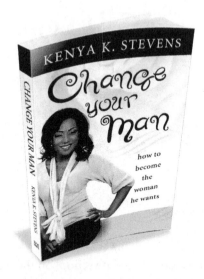

Change Your Man: How to Become the Woman He Wants

Learn the secrets of femininity and how to find true love in your life. Attract the man of your dreams by learning to change the inner you. Don't allow your inner man to stop you from attracting the man you've always desired. In this book, Kenya K. Stevens discusses the secrets she used to attract her husband and find true love.
Available on Amazon

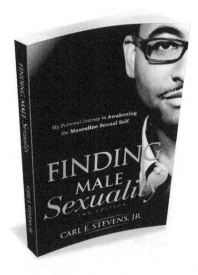

Finding Male Sexuality: My Personal Journey in Awakening the Masculine Sexual Self

Continue your learning experience by reading the second edition of *Finding Male Sexuality: My Personal Journey in Awakening the Masculine Sexual Self*. This book illustrates many of my sexual experiences that were critical in awakening my sexual power and skill as an effective lover to my many partners. Part 2 of the book gives practical exercises any man can use to awaken his sexual mastery.
Available on Amazon

The Art of Open Relating: Volume 1 – Theory, Philosophy, & Foundation

Continue your learning experience by reading *The Art of Open Relating: Volume 1: Theory, Philosophy, & Foundation* to expand your knowledge of open relating and alternative styles to love. Examine the additional relationship styles available and determine if a freedom-based relating model is right for you.

Available on Amazon

68590223R00118